Student Worktext

Transition

EAN#: 978-0-936785-40-0
ISBN#: 0-936785-40-3
TL#: HWSWTT2021WC

Published by Concerned Communications, LLC
P.O. Box 1000 • Siloam Springs, AR 72761

Authors	**Carol Ann Retzer**
	Eva Hoshino
Proofreaders	**Daniel Swatsenberg**
	Marcie Smith
Layout	**Mark Decker**
	Melissa Habermas
Illustrations	**Rob Harrell**
Colorists	**Josh & Aimee Ray**

Scripture translation selected for appropriate vocabulary level.
All verses are taken from *The Living Bible*, Tyndale House Publishers,
Wheaton, Illinois 60187. Used by permission.

Please, Help Us Hold Down Costs!

Photocopy machines are wonderful inventions, but did you know that it's ILLEGAL to reproduce copyrighted material?

Years of work and hundreds of thousands of dollars have gone into the development and production of **A Reason For Handwriting**®. Only your Christian integrity can help us avoid unnecessary price increases due to ILLEGAL photocopying.

Thank you for honoring copyright laws and not yielding to the temptation to "run off a few copies." It's not cost effective and it's ILLEGAL as well!

Attention Parents & Teachers:

Don't Settle for HALF a Curriculum!

A Reason For Handwriting® **Student Worktexts** integrate faith and learning by featuring lessons based on Scripture verses and built-in opportunities for sharing God's Word with others.

But, the **A Reason For Handwriting®** curriculum offers much, much more!

The **Comprehensive K-6th Teacher Guidebook** is full of essential instructions, helpful tips, and teacher-tested techniques to help you make the most of your handwriting practice.

Key instructional information in the **Teacher Guidebook** includes:

- **The Suggested Weekly Schedule**
- **Daily Lesson Plans**
- **Tips for Teaching Cursive Handwriting**
- **Techniques for Grading**

Plus the **Teacher Guidebook** includes a wealth of teacher-tested tips and enrichment ideas:

- **A Comprehesive Skills Index**
- **Extended Activities**
- **Ways to Share Border Sheets**
- **Letter Formation Charts**
- **Tips for Proper Positioning**
- **Letter Group Charts**
- **Vocabulary Lists**
- **Common Handwriting Problems**
- **Black Line Masters**

To order the **A Reason For Handwriting®** K-6th **Teacher Guidebook**
that goes with this **Student Worktext**, contact your curriculum supplier
or call 800.447.4332

Or go to:
www.AReasonFor.com

Just For Kids!

Welcome to A Reason For Handwriting®

This year you'll learn to write better, memorize Scripture, share God's Word, and have FUN!

Each week you'll practice letters and groups of letters from a different Scripture verse. Then you'll write the entire verse on practice paper. At the end of each week you'll pick a Scripture Border Sheet from the back of your Worktext,

Parker

Susan

Rodney

write the verse in your very best handwriting, and use your creative talents to color and decorate it. Now comes the really FUN part: Sharing God's Word!

You can share God's Word, in your very own handwriting, by giving people your finished Scripture Border Sheets! You can take them to nursing homes, share them with friends, make placemats for your kitchen table, mail them to someone who isn't feeling well. . . you get the idea. And we're sure you'll come up with even more ideas throughout the year!

And sharing God's Word with others gives you the very best reason for improving your handwriting!

Meet New Friends

Throughout this book, you'll see illustrations of kids like you who are caring, sharing, working, and learning. Be sure to watch for these new faces!

Rachel

Greg

Alli

Jared

Kes

How to Become A Five Star Student!

Here are five basic areas to consider when evaluating your handwriting form:

 Alignment

Each letter should sit *on* the line, not above or below it.

 Slant

The letter slant should be uniform and consistent. (To help you determine direction, draw a line straight down the middle of each letter in a sentence.)

 Size

Manuscript: Capital letters are all one full space tall. The lowercase letters b, d, f, h, k, l, and t are also one space tall. All other lowercase letters are half a space tall. Also, tail letters (g, j, p, q, and y) should extend to the bottom line.

Cursive: Capital letters are all one full space tall. The lowercase letters *b, d, f, h, k, l* and *t* are also one space tall. All other lowercase letters are half a space tall. Also, any letter that goes below the line should extend for half a space.

 Shape

Letters should be consistent and easy to read. Minor differences from the model are okay, but all your letters must be formed with the proper strokes to avoid developing bad habits.

 Spacing

Letters should be clearly identifiable. They should not run into each other, or be too far apart. Each word should be separated from the next word. Remember, a little more space is needed between sentences than between words.

Practice the following sentence in both manuscript and cursive. It contains all the letters of the alphabet.

God created zebras and foxes to walk, jump, and hide very quickly.

God created zebras and foxes to walk, jump, and hide very quickly.

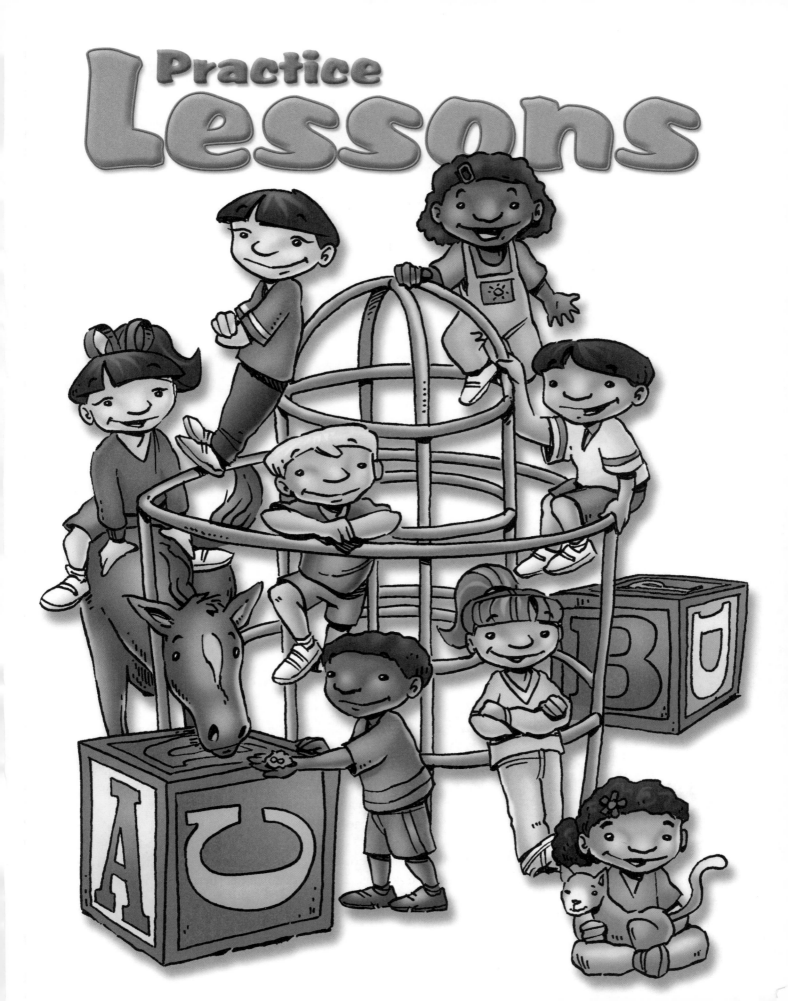

To The Teacher

After the summer break, students often benefit from a focused review. The following Practice Lessons provide a quick, efficient method for reviewing manuscript letter formation. These lessons are designed for one page each day, for a total of 10 days.

Before beginning this section, please review Making The Transition (Teacher Guidebook, page 232) for detailed instructions on how to use this Student Worktext.

Name _____

Aa Bb Cc Dd Ee Ff
Gg Hh Ii Jj Kk Ll Mm
Nn Oo Pp Qq Rr Ss
Tt Uu Vv Ww Xx Yy
Zz 0 1 2 3 4 5 6 7 8 9

 c

 o

 a

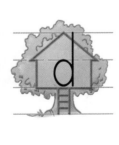 d

 e

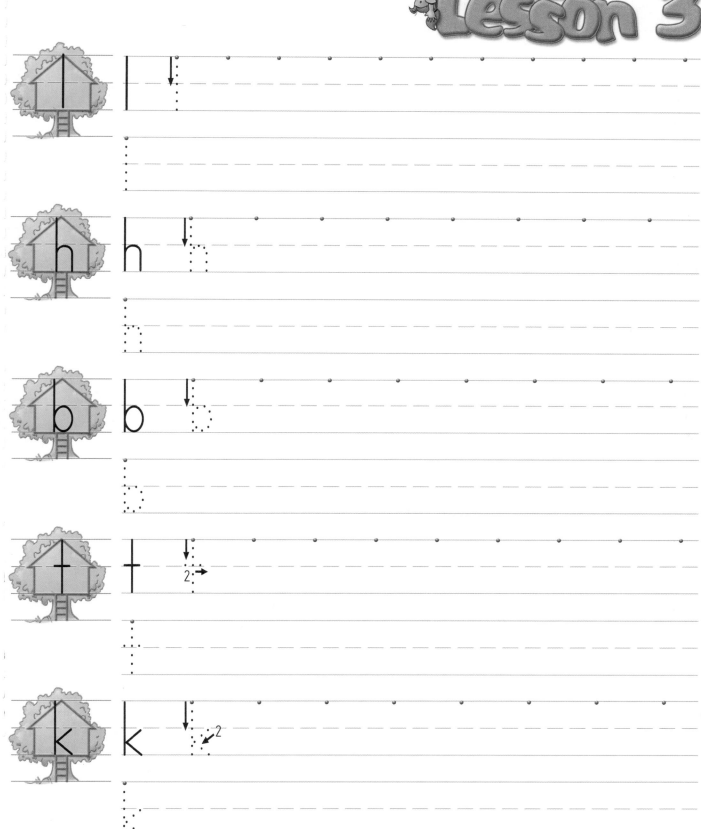

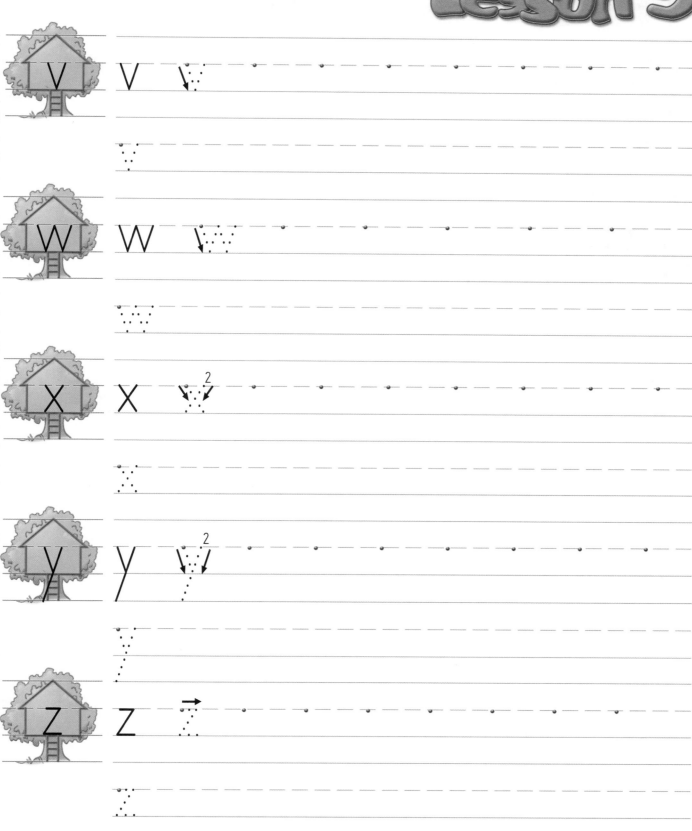

 r   r   r

 n   n   n

 m   m   m

 s   s   s

 u   u   u

Name _____

p   p

q   q

y   y

g   g

j   j

C C C · · · · ·

O O O · · · · ·

G G G · · · · ·

Q Q Q · · · · ·

P P P · · · · ·

R R R · · · · ·

B B B · · · · ·

D D D · · · · ·

God is good!

Praise the Lord!

A

X

M

N

K

V

W

Y

Z

You are very special.

Name

Practice
Lesson 10

I I I

L L L

T T T

F F F

E E E

H H H

J J J

U U U

S S S

Jesus loves me!

18

Manuscript Lessons

To The Teacher

Before beginning this section, please review **Making The Transition** (Teacher Guidebook, page 232), and the **Weekly Lesson Format** (Teacher Guidebook, page 56).

Making The Transition gives detailed instructions on how to use this book, based on when your school makes the transition from manuscript to cursive handwriting.

The **Weekly Lesson Format** provides detailed directions for implementing the 5-day format, as well as suggestions for using the **Scripture Border Sheets**. Careful review of this material at the start of the school year will greatly enhance the effectiveness of this curriculum.

Name_____

TIP OF THE WEEK

Manuscript handwriting is a skill
you will use for the rest of your life. This year,
we'll be sharing ways to make your handwriting even better!

Day One Practice the following letters and words from this week's Scripture.

Aa

Dd

and

Day Two Continue practicing letters and words from this week's Scripture.

all

heart

Lord Lord

God God

mind mind

Love the Lord your God with all your heart, soul, and mind. Matthew 22:37

The letter **o** forms one part of the
letter **g** — can you see it? Write both of these
letters in one stroke, without picking up your pencil.

Day One   Practice the following letters and words from this week's Scripture.

Gg

Oo

go

Day Two   Continue practicing letters and words from this week's Scripture.

greatness

for

care care

of of

measure measure

Your care for others is the measure of your greatness. Luke 9:48

Name _____

Your name is important — just like you!
Write your letters carefully. Make certain
they are the correct size and sit firmly on the line.

Day One   Practice the following letters and words from this week's Scripture.

Qq

Uu

quickly

Day Two   Continue practicing letters and words from this week's Scripture.

Come

terms

Day Three

Practice the final letters and words from this week's Scripture.

before before

late late

too too

Day Four

Practice this week's entire Scripture verse by tracing over each of the letters below.

Come to terms quickly
before it is too late.
Matthew 5:25

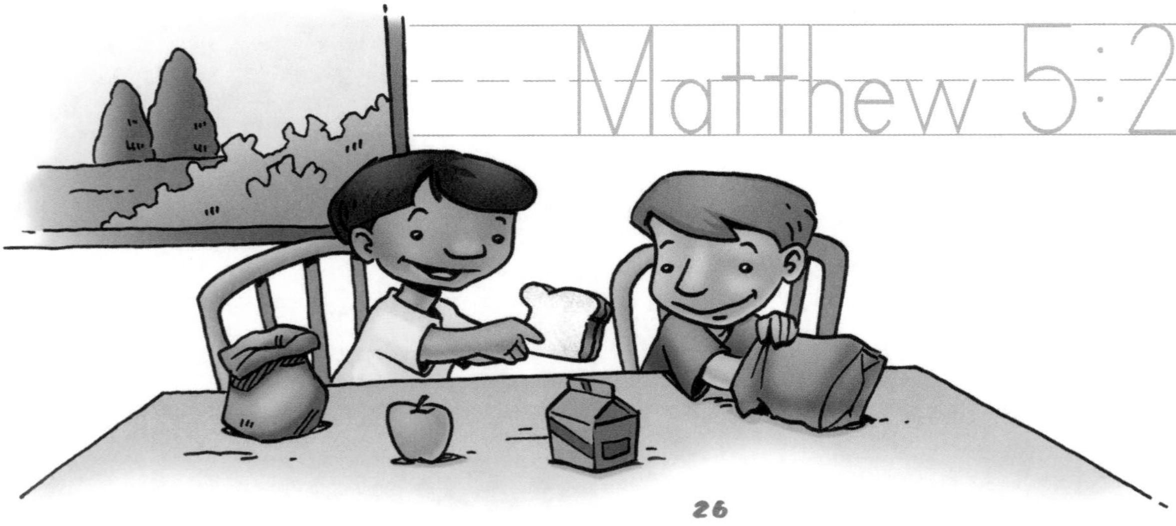

Name _____

TIP OF THE WEEK

How are the lowercase **c** and **e** alike?
How are they different? As you write these
letters, make sure that they fill the entire space.

Day One   Practice the following letters and words from this week's Scripture.

Cc Cc

Ee Ee

each each

Day Two   Continue practicing letters and words from this week's Scripture.

peace peace

Live Live

Day Three

other   other

in   in

with   with

Day Four

Live in peace with each other. Mark 9:50

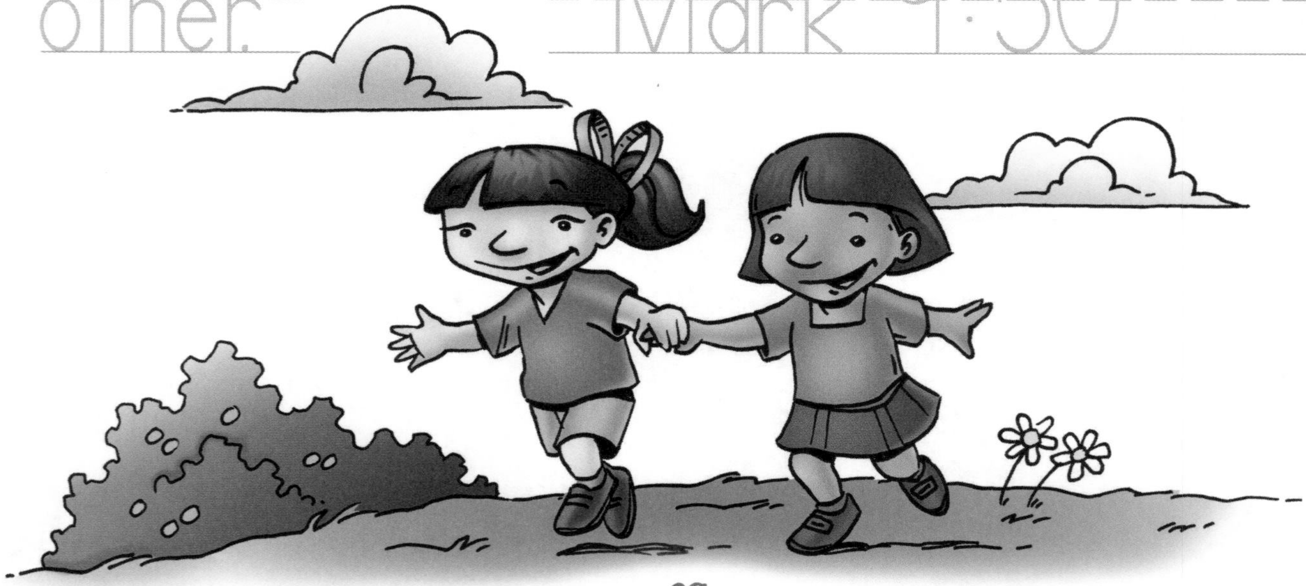

28

TIP OF THE WEEK

How are the lowercase **b** and **p**
different? How are they alike? Be sure
the tail of the **p** goes all the way to the ground.

Day One   Practice the following letters and words from this week's Scripture.

Bb

Pp

prepare

Day Two   Continue practicing letters and words from this week's Scripture.

coming

Be

Day Three

Practice the final letters and words from this week's Scripture.

don't don't

prepared prepared

know know

Day Four

Practice this week's entire Scripture verse by tracing over each of the letters below.

Be prepared, for you don't know what day your Lord is coming. Matthew 24:42

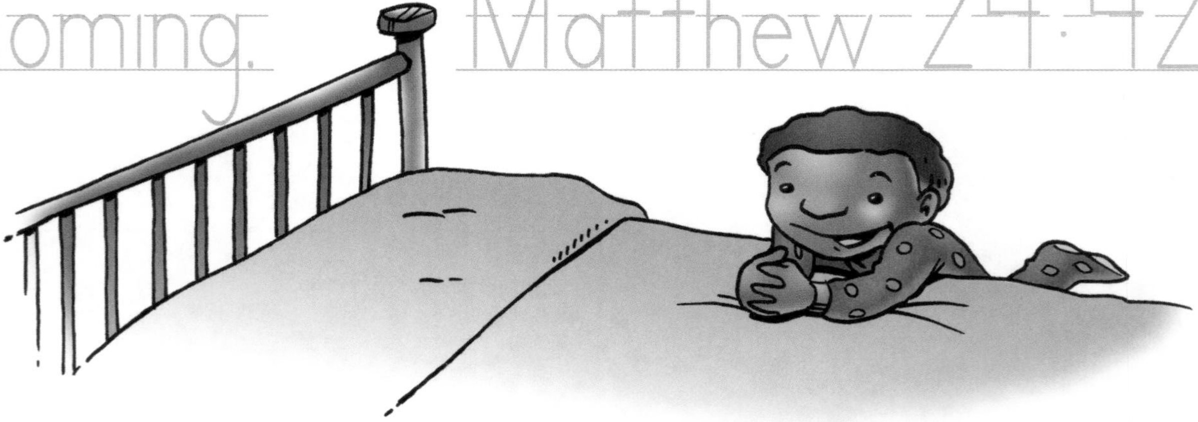

Name _____

TIP OF THE WEEK

Are your letters and words sitting
firmly on the line? Think of your letters
as birds sitting on a wire. Don't let them fall off!

Day One   Practice the following letters and words from this week's Scripture.

Ll   Ll

Vv   Vv

love   love

Day Two   Continue practicing letters and words from this week's Scripture.

prove   prove

will   will

strong strong

disciples disciples

world world

Day Four Practice this week's entire Scripture verse by tracing over each of the letters below.

Your strong love for each

other will prove to the world

that you are my disciples.

John 13:35

TIP OF THE WEEK

Who was Mark, and why will you be
writing his name this week? Other names this
year are Matthew, Luke, and John. Who were they?

Day One   Practice the following letters and words from this week's Scripture.

Mm

Nn

done

Day Two   Continue practicing letters and words from this week's Scripture.

things

them

Mark   Mark

wonderful   wonderful

home   home

Day Four   Practice this week's entire Scripture verse by tracing over each of the letters below.

Go home to your friends, and tell them what wonderful things God has done for you.

Mark 5:19

TIP OF THE WEEK

Think of how you have to stretch to reach
the top shelf. This week, help your tall letters
(d, f, h, l, and t) stretch all the way to the top line.

Day One   Practice the following letters and words from this week's Scripture.

Ff

Hh

filled

Day Two   Continue practicing letters and words from this week's Scripture.

light

within

face   face

then   then

radiant   radiant

Day Four Practice this week's entire Scripture verse by tracing over each of the letters below.

If you are filled with light within, then your face will be radiant too. Luke 11:36

 **TIP OF THE WEEK**

Two lowercase letters that are almost look-alikes are i and j. Remember, the j has a tail just like a monkey. Don't forget to dot both letters.

Day One   Practice the following letters and words from this week's Scripture.

I i

J j

rejoice

Day Two   Continue practicing letters and words from this week's Scripture.

praise

how

Savior Savior

my my

Oh Oh

Oh, how I praise the Lord.
How I rejoice in God my
Savior! Luke 1:46, 47

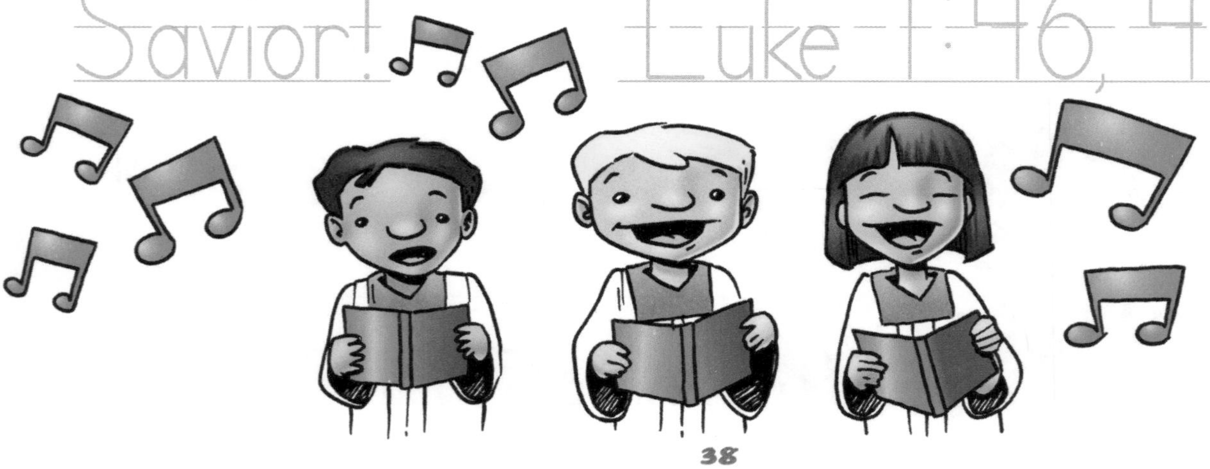

Name _____

 **TIP OF THE WEEK**

The lowercase **y** is one of the two-stroke letters. How many other two-stroke letters can you find in this week's verse?

Day One   Practice the following letters and words from this week's Scripture.

Uu   Uu

Yy   Yy

you   you

Day Two   Continue practicing letters and words from this week's Scripture.

your   your

much   much

yourself   yourself

neighbor   neighbor

as   as

Love your neighbor as much as you love yourself. Matthew 22:39

Lesson 11

📚 **TIP OF THE WEEK**

The capital R begins with a straight downstroke.
The capital W is written with all slanting lines. Sit
straight like the R as you write your words this week.

Day One Practice the following letters and words from this week's Scripture.

Rr

Ww

words

Day Two Continue practicing letters and words from this week's Scripture.

away

remain

earth   earth

true   true

forever   forever

Day Four Practice this week's entire Scripture verse by tracing over each of the letters below.

Though all heaven and earth shall pass away, yet My words remain forever true.

Luke 21:33

42

TIP OF THE WEEK

How are you holding your pencil?
Is it sharp? It is much easier to write well
when you hold your pencil correctly and it is sharp!

Day One   Practice the following letters and words from this week's Scripture.

Kk   Kk

Xx   Xx

make   make

Day Two   Continue practicing letters and words from this week's Scripture.

exists   exists

created   created

Day Three
Practice the final letters and words from this week's Scripture.

nothing   nothing

everything   everything

didn't   didn't

Day Four
Practice this week's entire Scripture verse by tracing over each of the letters below.

He created everything
there is—nothing exists that
He didn't make.
John 1:3

Name _____

📖 **TIP OF THE WEEK**

The capital T and lowercase t
both have a cross, but in different
places. Watch where you cross the lowercase t.

Day One   Practice the following letters and words from this week's Scripture.

Ss

Tt

wants

Day Two   Continue practicing letters and words from this week's Scripture.

take

cross

let let

anyone anyone

mine mine

Day Four Practice this week's entire Scripture verse by tracing over each of the letters below.

If anyone wants to be a follower of mine, let him take up his cross and follow Me. Matthew 16:24

Name _____

TIP OF THE WEEK

Make certain your letters are all
the correct size and that they fill the space
completely! This makes your writing easier to read.

Day One   Practice the following letters and words from this week's Scripture.

Cc

Zz

come

Day Two   Continue practicing letters and words from this week's Scripture.

criticize

back

condemn condemn

on on

Never Never

Never criticize or condemn—
or it will all come back on you.
Luke 6:37

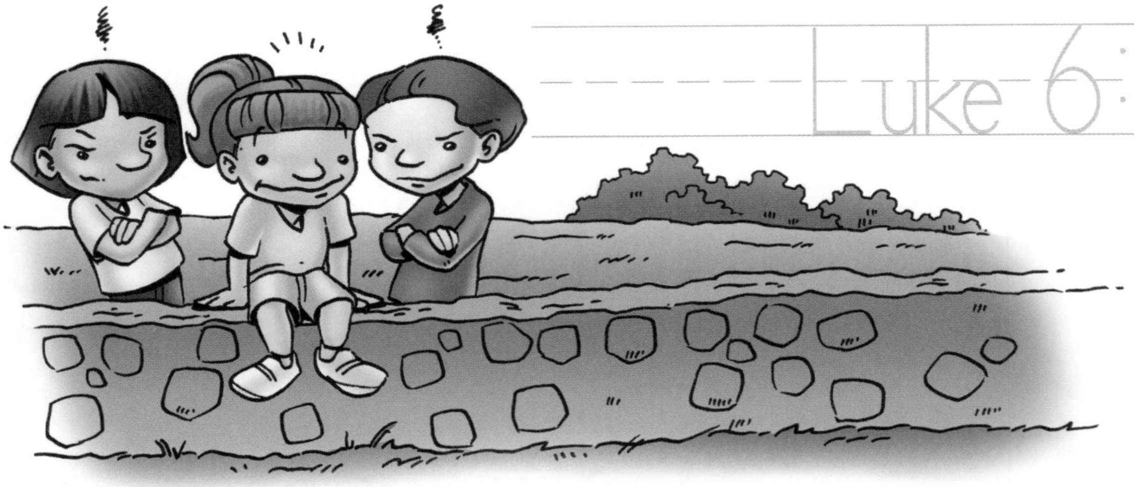

Name _____

As you write the lowercase **b**,
be sure to start at the top! Tell a
friend exactly how to make this letter.

Day One Practice the following letters and words from this week's Scripture.

Bb   Bb

Oo   Oo

who   who

Day Two Continue practicing letters and words from this week's Scripture.

bring   bring

followers   followers

world   world

truth   truth

came   came

Day Four Practice this week's entire Scripture verse by tracing over each of the letters below.

I came to bring truth to the world. All who love the truth are My followers. John 18:37

Name _____

TIP OF THE WEEK

Two of this week's focus letters
are capital and lowercase look-alikes: the S
and s; the W and w. See how the S slithers around?

Day One   Practice the following letters and words from this week's Scripture.

S s

W w

So

Day Two   Continue practicing letters and words from this week's Scripture.

worship

written

Scriptures Scriptures

We We

must must

We must worship God, and Him alone. So it is written in the Scriptures. Luke 4:8

Name _____

TIP OF THE WEEK

Make good, straight lines for the
downstrokes on the capital E, H, L, and P.
All these letters are found in this week's lesson.

Day One   Practice the following letters and words from this week's Scripture.

E e   E e

P p   P p

people   people

Day Two   Continue practicing letters and words from this week's Scripture.

Praise   Praise

He   He

them them

redeemed redeemed

visit visit

Day Four Practice this week's entire Scripture verse by tracing over each of the letters below.

Praise the Lord, for He has come to visit His people and has redeemed them.

Luke 1:68

Name _____

 **TIP OF THE WEEK**

Look around your classroom for a sign
that contains the letter **X**. (Here's a clue:
It should be by the door where you go out.)

Day One Practice the following letters and words from this week's Scripture.

Vv V v

Xx X x

exit exit

Day Two Continue practicing letters and words from this week's Scripture.

always always

even even

end   end

with   with

the   the

I am with you always, even
to the end of the world.
Matthew 28:20

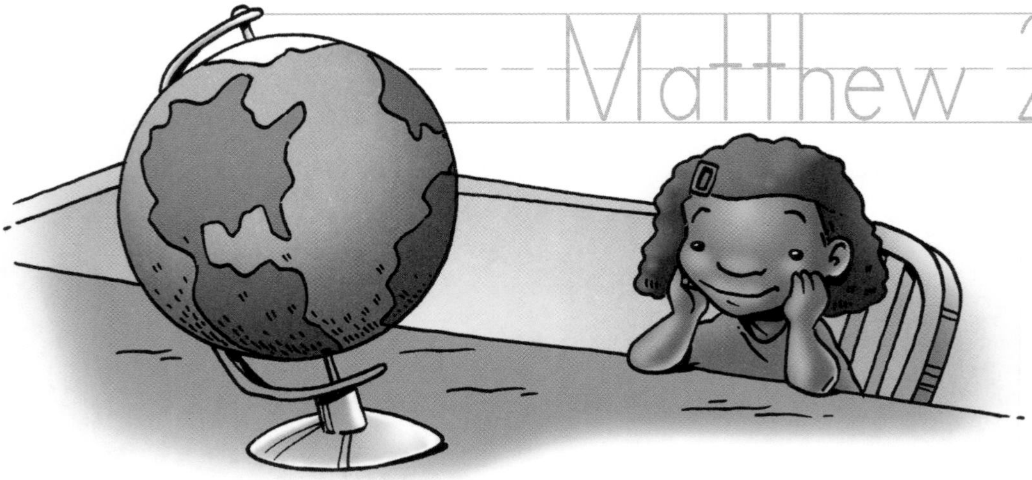

TIP OF THE WEEK

The capital letter A is a three-
stroke letter. So are the letters E, F, H, and I.
Count the strokes as you write these letters this week.

Day One
Practice the following letters and words from this week's Scripture.

Aa Aa

Ll Ll

at at

Day Two
Continue practicing letters and words from this week's Scripture.

day day

Live Live

time

one

tomorrow

God will take care of your tomorrow. Live one day at a time. Matthew 6:34

Name _____

TIP OF THE WEEK

If your hand gets tired while
you are writing, you may be holding
your pencil too tightly. Try to loosen up a bit!

Day One   Practice the following letters and words from this week's Scripture.

Tt

Gg

get

Day Two   Continue practicing letters and words from this week's Scripture.

angels

There

Day Three — Practice the final letters and words from this week's Scripture.

presence   presence

repents   repents

when   when

Day Four — Practice this week's entire Scripture verse by tracing over each of the letters below.

There is joy in the presence of the angels of God when one sinner repents.

Luke 15:10

 **TIP OF THE WEEK**

Some letters are tall, some have tails, and some sit in the middle. But even though your letters are different, they should all be the correct size.

Day One   Practice the following letters and words from this week's Scripture.

I i

Z z

size

Day Two   Continue practicing letters and words from this week's Scripture.

practice

into

listen   listen

ears   ears

sure   sure

Day Four Practice this week's entire Scripture verse by tracing over each of the letters below.

If you have ears, listen!

Be sure to put into practice

what you hear.

Mark 4:23, 24

Tip of the Week

Using your index finger, outline a
letter on a friend's back. See if they can tell
what you wrote. Now trade places and try it again.

Day One   Practice the following letters and words from this week's Scripture.

Hh

Yy

Holy

Day Two   Continue practicing letters and words from this week's Scripture.

heavenly

Father

Your   Your

those   those

ask   ask

Your heavenly Father will give the Holy Spirit to those who ask for Him.

Luke 11:13

Name _____

TIP OF THE WEEK

How are the capital B and R alike?
How are they different? Name some
people whose name begins with a B or R.

Day One   Practice the following letters and words from this week's Scripture.

Bb   Bb

Rr   Rr

are   are

Day Two   Continue practicing letters and words from this week's Scripture.

bless   bless

Word   Word

Day Three — Practice the final letters and words from this week's Scripture.

Blessed   Blessed

who   who

hear   hear

Day Four — Practice this week's entire Scripture verse by tracing over each of the letters below.

Blessed are all who hear the Word of God and put it into practice.

Luke 11:28

Name _____

 **TIP OF THE WEEK**

Writing is easier if your paper is slanted
the same way as your writing arm. This is true
not only in handwriting, but in your other subjects as well.

Day One   Practice the following letters and words from this week's Scripture.

Aa   Aa

Dd   Dd

Do   Do

Day Two   Continue practicing letters and words from this week's Scripture.

want   want

what   what

to

do

others

Do for others what you want them to do for you. Matthew 7:12

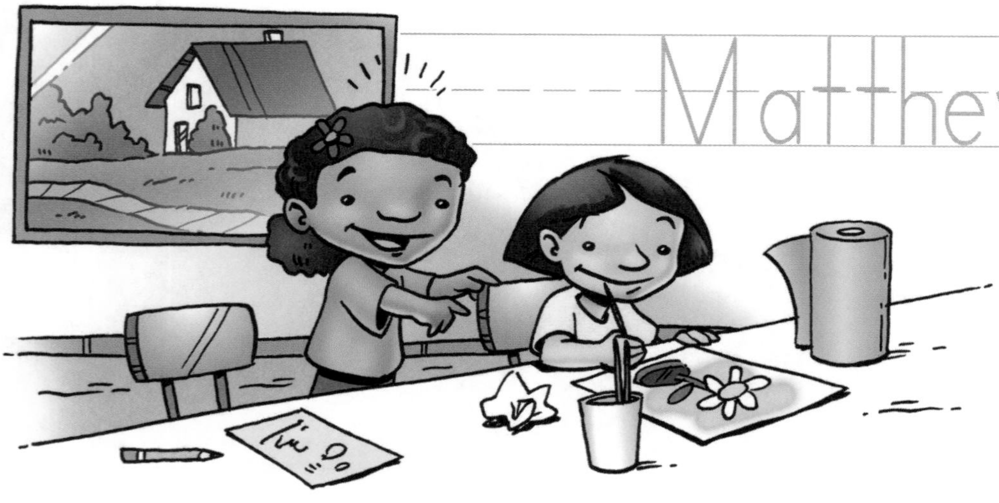

If you made a lowercase **g** with a pipe
cleaner or clay, how would you turn it into a **q**?
Write these letters without picking up your pencil.

Day One   Practice the following letters and words from this week's Scripture.

Gg

Qq

quit

Day Two   Continue practicing letters and words from this week's Scripture.

blessings

God

give ~give~

ready ~ready~

Him ~Him~

Day Four   Practice this week's entire Scripture verse by tracing over each of the letters below.

God is ready to give blessings to all who come to Him. Luke 4:19

Name _____

 **TIP OF THE WEEK**

When you sit up straight, it is easier to
write and your handwriting improves. When your
letters "sit up straight" on the line, they are easier to read.

Day One   Practice the following letters and words from this week's Scripture.

Ee   Ee

Tt   Tt

set   set

Day Two   Continue practicing letters and words from this week's Scripture.

free   free

You   You

truth   truth

know   know

will   will

You will know the truth, and
the truth will set you free.
John 8:32

72

Name _____

TIP OF THE WEEK

Two letters in this verse are crossed
at the mid-line after the downstroke. Can
you find them? (Here's a clue: both are tall letters.)

Day One   Practice the following letters and words from this week's Scripture.

Ff

Mm

from

Day Two   Continue practicing letters and words from this week's Scripture.

friends

Matthew

friendly   friendly

different   different

else   else

If you are friendly only to
your friends, how are you
different from anyone else?
Matthew 5:47

To The Teacher

Before beginning this section, please review To The Teacher (Teacher Guidebook, page 115-116), and Making The Transition (Teacher Guidebook, page 232).

Making The Transition gives detailed instructions on how to use this book, based on when your school makes the transition from manuscript to cursive handwriting.

Careful review of To The Teacher at the start of the school year will greatly enhance the effectiveness of this curriculum.

Practice Your Name

Āā 𝒶𝒶

𝒶𝒶

Ā 𝒶

𝒶

ā 𝒶

𝒶

āaa 𝒶𝒶𝒶

𝒶𝒶𝒶

Focus Letter E e *Ee*

Transition Lesson 2

Practice Your Name

Ee Ee

Ee

E E

E

e e

e

eee eee

eee

Practice Your Name

I i   *Ii*

Practice Your Name

𝒪𝑜 𝒪𝑜

𝒪𝑜

𝒪

𝒪

𝑜

𝑜

𝑜𝑜𝑜

𝑜𝑜𝑜

 **Focus Letter** Uu *Uu*

 **Transition** **Lesson 5**

Practice Your Name

Uu Uu

Uu

U U

U

u u

u

uuuuu uuuuu

uuuuu

Practice Your Name

Bb Bb

Bb

B B

B

b b

b

bbb bbb

bbb

Practice Your Name

Ĉĉ Cc

Cc

Ĉ C

C

ĉ c

c

ĉcc ccc

ccc

Focus Letter Dd Dd

Practice Your Name

D d   D d

D d

D   D

d   d

ddd   ddd

Practice Your Name

Practice Your Name

$\mathcal{G}$ $\bar{g}$ $\mathcal{G}$ g

$\mathcal{G}$ g

$\mathcal{G}$ $\mathcal{G}$

$\mathcal{G}$

$\bar{g}$ g

g

$\bar{g}gg$ ggg

ggg

Practice Your Name

𝓗𝓱 𝓗𝓱

𝓗𝓱

𝓗 𝓗

𝓗

𝓱 𝓱

𝓱

𝓱𝓱𝓱 𝓱𝓱𝓱

𝓱𝓱𝓱

Focus Letter J j *J j*

Practice Your Name

Focus Letter Kk *Kk*

Practice Your Name

$\mathcal{K}$ *k* $\mathcal{K}k$

$\mathcal{K}k$

$\mathcal{K}$ $\mathcal{K}$

$\mathcal{K}$

k *k*

k

kkk *kkk*

kkk

Practice Your Name

$\mathcal{L}\ \ell\quad \mathcal{L}\ell$

$\mathcal{L}\ell$

$\mathcal{L}\qquad \mathcal{L}$

$\mathcal{L}$

$\ell\qquad \ell$

ℓ

$\ell\ell\ell\qquad \ell\ell\ell$

$\ell\ell\ell$

 Focus Letter Mm 𝓜𝓶

Practice Your Name

𝓜 𝓶   𝓜 𝓶

𝓜 𝓶

𝓜   𝓜

𝓜

𝓶   𝓶

𝓶

𝓶𝓶𝓶   𝓶𝓶𝓶

𝓶𝓶𝓶

Focus Letter Nn 𝑁𝑛

Practice Your Name

𝑁𝑛 𝑁𝑛

𝑁𝑛

𝑁 𝑁

𝑁

𝑚 𝑚

𝑚

𝑚𝑛𝑛 𝑚𝑛𝑛

𝑚𝑛𝑛

Practice Your Name

𝒫 𝓅   𝒫 𝓅

𝒫 𝓅

𝒫   𝒫

𝒫

𝓅   𝓅

𝓅

𝓅𝓅𝓅   𝓅𝓅𝓅

𝓅𝓅𝓅

Focus Letter Qq Qq

Practice Your Name

Q q Q q

Q q

Q Q

Q

q q

q

q q q q q q

q q q

Practice Your Name

ℛ𝓇 ℛ𝓇

ℛ𝓇

ℛ ℛ

ℛ

𝓇 𝓇

𝓇

𝓇𝓇𝓇 𝓇𝓇𝓇

𝓇𝓇𝓇

Practice Your Name

𝒮s

s

𝒮

s

s

s

sss

Practice Your Name

Focus Letter V v 𝒱𝓋

Practice Your Name

𝒱𝓋 𝒱𝓋

𝒱𝓋

𝒱 𝒱

𝒱

𝓋 𝓋

𝓋

𝓋𝓋𝓋 𝓋𝓋𝓋

𝓋𝓋𝓋

Focus Letter W w *Ww*

Practice Your Name

Ww   Ww

Ww

W   W

W

w   w

w

www   www

www

 Xx 𝒳𝓍

 Transition **Lesson 24**

Practice Your Name

𝒳 𝒳𝓍 𝒳𝓍

𝒳𝓍

𝒳 𝒳

𝒳

𝓍 𝓍

𝓍

𝓍𝓍𝓍 𝓍𝓍𝓍

𝓍𝓍𝓍

Practice Your Name

Yy Yy

Yy

Y Y

Y

y y

y

yyy yyy

yyy

Practice Your Name →

102

Transition Lesson 27

Practice Your Name

e e

i i

l l

h h

k k

kkk kkk

help help

help

Practice Your Name

o   o

o

a   a

a

c   c

c

d   d

d

ddd   ddd

coal   coal

coal

Practice Your Name

ḡ   g

g

q̄   q

q

p   p

p

ḡood   good

equip   equip

ḡold   gold

105

Practice Your Name

i   *i*

i

u   *u*

u

w   *w*

w

with   *with*

quick   *quick*

will   *will*

Practice Your Name

j   *j*

j

f   *f*

f

t   *t*

t

jump   *jump*

fit   *fit*

jet   *jet*

Practice Your Name

r   n   .   .   .   .

n

s   s   .   .   .   .

s

b   b   .   .   .   .

b

right   right   .   .   .

sure   sure   .   .   .

boat   boat   .   .   .

Lesson 33

Practice Your Name →

m m

m

m m

m

n n

n

men men

jam jam

verse verse

Practice Your Name

x^2 *a*

a

ny   *y*

y

nz   *z*

z

year   *year*

zebra   *zebra*

exit   *exit*

Practice Your Name

Āā Aa

Ā A

āaa aaa

Ōō Oo

Ō O

ōoo ooo

Ābba Abba

Ādam Adam

Òbadiah Obadiah

Òmega Omega

Practice Your Name

$\hat{C}\hat{c}$ Cc

$\hat{C}$ C

$\hat{c}cc$ ccc

$\hat{E}e$ Ee

$\hat{E}$ E

eee eee

$\hat{C}aleb$ $Caleb$

$\hat{C}anaan$ $Canaan$

$\hat{E}sther$ $Esther$

$\hat{E}ve$ Eve

Practice Your Name

𝒢g Gg

𝒢 G

ggg ggg

𝒮s Ss

𝒮 S

sss sss

𝒯t Tt

𝒯 T

ttt ttt

God God

Son Son

Timothy Timothy

Practice Your Name

ℐi   ℐi

ℐ   ℐ

iii   iii

ℐj   ℐj

ℐ

jjj   jjj

Q q   Q q

Q   Q

qqq   qqq

Isaac   Isaac

Jesus   Jesus

Queen   Queen

Practice Your Name

H h   Hh

H   H

hhh   hhh

K k   Kk

K   K

kkk   kkk

X x   Xx

X   X

xxx   xxx

Hebrews   Hebrews

Kingdom   Kingdom

Xerxes   Xerxes

Practice Your Name

M m   M m

M   M

mmm   mmm

N m   N n

N   N

mnn   mnn

U u   U u

U   U

uuu   uuu

Messiah   Messiah

Numbers   Numbers

Ur   Ur

Practice Your Name

F f   F f

F   F

fff   fff

U u   Uu

U   U

uuu   uuu

W w   Wu

W   W

uuuu   uuuu

Father   Father

Victory   Victory

Worship   Worship

117

Transition Lesson 42

𝒟 𝒹 𝒟𝒹

𝒟 𝒟

𝒹𝒹𝒹 𝒹𝒹𝒹

ℒ ℓ ℒℓ

ℒ ℒ

ℓℓℓ ℓℓℓ

Daniel Daniel

David David

Lazarus Lazarus

Lord Lord

Practice Your Name →

P p   P p

P   P

ppp   ppp

R r   R r

R   R

rrr   rrr

B b   B b

B   B

bbb   bbb

Bible   Bible

Paul   Paul

Ruth   Ruth

Practice Your Name

𝒴 𝓎   𝒴 𝓎
𝒴   𝒴

𝓎𝓎𝓎   𝓎𝓎𝓎
ℨ 𝓏   ℨ 𝓏
ℨ   ℨ

𝓏𝓏𝓏   𝓏𝓏𝓏
Yoke   Yoke

You   You

Zacchaeus   Zacchaeus

Zion   Zion

Practice Your Name

Aā Bb Cc Dd Ee Ff Gg
Hh Ii Jj Kk Ll Mm
Nn Oo Pp Qq Rr Ss Tt
Uu Vv Ww Xx Yy Zz
1 2 3 4 5 6 7 8 9 0

To The Teacher

Before beginning this section, please review Making The Transition (Teacher Guidebook, page 232), and the **Weekly Lesson Format** (Teacher Guidebook, page 56).

Making The Transition gives detailed instructions on how to use this book, based on when your school makes the transition from manuscript to cursive handwriting.

The **Weekly Lesson Format** provides detailed directions for implementing the 5-day format, as well as suggestions for using the Scripture Border Sheets. Careful review of this material at the start of the school year will greatly enhance the effectiveness of this curriculum.

 **Tip of the week**

As you get taller and smarter this year, make sure
your handwriting grows, too! Strive to be a **Five Star** student.
(See page 6.) Good handwriting helps others read what you have to say.

Day One   Practice the following letters and words from this week's Scripture.

Dd

God

good

began

Day Two   Continue practicing letters and words from this week's Scripture.

Oo

grow

work

who

Day Three
Practice the final letters and words from this week's Scripture.

Yy

you

grace

will

Day Four
Practice this week's entire Scripture verse by tracing over each of the words below.

God who began the good work within you will keep right on helping you grow in His grace.
Philippians 1:6

FOR DISCUSSION

How much have you grown since last year? Is physical growth the only way we can grow? What do you think it means to "grow in God's grace?"

TIP OF THE WEEK

Close your eyes and picture the strokes for the capital
and lowercase *A a*, *E e*, and *J j*. With your eyes still closed,
write these six letters with your index finger on the palm of your other hand.

Day One Practice the following letters and words from this week's Scripture.

A a

mind

Father

great

Day Two Continue practicing letters and words from this week's Scripture.

E e

peace

May

blessings

Day Three
Practice the final letters and words from this week's Scripture.

Jj

Jesus

give

heart

Day Four
Practice this week's entire Scripture verse by tracing over each of the words below.

May God our Father and the
Lord Jesus Christ give you all of
His blessings, and great peace of
heart and mind.

I Corinthians 1:3

FOR DISCUSSION
Make a list of some "blessings" that make you happy. Now compare your list with a friend's. How are they similar? How are they different?

TIP OF THE WEEK

Letters are different heights, just like people! Some
lowercase letters fill only half the space, while tall letters
(*b*, *d*, *f*, *h*, *k*, *l*, and *t*) fill the whole space, and touch the top lines.

Day One Practice the following letters and words from this week's Scripture.

Rr

worry

pray

answers

Day Two Continue practicing letters and words from this week's Scripture.

Tt

tell

anything

thank

Uu

your

Don't

instead

Day Four   Practice this week's entire Scripture verse by tracing over each of the words below.

Don't worry about anything; instead, pray about everything; tell God your needs and don't forget to thank Him for His answers.

Philippians 4:6

FOR DISCUSSION

Does God always answer prayers with a "yes?" What other answers might God give? Why?

TIP OF THE WEEK

When you tie your shoes, you make loops for the bows.
When you write some letters, you make loops, too! Make certain
the loops in *b, e, f, h, k,* and *l* are open — but don't put loops in *t* or *d.*

Day One Practice the following letters and words from this week's Scripture.

Bb

be

about

dwell

Day Two Continue practicing letters and words from this week's Scripture.

Ll

glad

all

think

Pp

praise

Philippians

fine

Day Four Practice this week's entire Scripture verse by tracing over each of the words below.

Dwell on the fine, good things in others. Think about all you can praise God for and be glad about. — Philippians 4:8

FOR DISCUSSION

What are some of the "fine, good things" that you can see in your classmates? Which of these traits would you like to have, too?

TIP OF THE WEEK

The capitals *G* and *S* are "boatstroke" capitals.
The other boatstroke capitals are *B, F, I,* and *T.*
Remember, boatstroke capitals are not joined to the rest of the word.

Day One Practice the following letters and words from this week's Scripture.

Gg

God

anyone

that

Day Two Continue practicing letters and words from this week's Scripture.

Ss

Son

says

believes

Day Three   Practice the final letters and words from this week's Scripture.

Un

living

him

is

Day Four   Practice this week's entire Scripture verse by tracing over each of the words below.

Anyone who believes and says that Jesus is the Son of God has God living in him, and he is living with God.

I John 4:15

FOR DISCUSSION

When God is living in our hearts, how does this affect our behavior? Name some traits that might show we are "living with God."

134

Name _____

TIP OF THE WEEK

Is your hand getting tired as you write? You may
be holding your pencil incorrectly, or too tightly. Have your
teacher check your pencil position. Relax your wrist by rotating it in a circle.

Day One   Practice the following letters and words from this week's Scripture.

Cc

can

Christ

asks

Day Two   Continue practicing letters and words from this week's Scripture.

Hh

Help

strength

the

Ww

who

power

with

Day Four   Practice this week's entire Scripture verse by tracing over each of the words below.

I can do everything God asks me to with the help of Christ who gives me the strength and power. Philippians 4:13

FOR DISCUSSION

What sort of things might God ask you to do? How does this verse say we should get the "strength and power" to do them?

TIP OF THE WEEK

There are four lowercase letters (*i, j, t,* and *x*) that require an extra stroke after the word is written. Pay close attention to these letters as you practice.

Day One Practice the following letters and words from this week's Scripture.

Ii

forgiving

forgiven

just

Day Two Continue practicing letters and words from this week's Scripture.

Kk

kind

has

each

Day Three — Practice the final letters and words from this week's Scripture.

Ft

tenderhearted

another

other

Day Four — Practice this week's entire Scripture verse by tracing over each of the words below.

Be kind to each other,
tenderhearted, forgiving one another,
just as God has forgiven you.
Ephesians 4:32

FOR DISCUSSION

List some ways you can show kindness to your classmates. . .your family. . .your neighbors. Try to put at least one of these ideas into action this week.

📚 TIP OF THE WEEK

The bridgestroke family includes
the lowercase *b*, *o*, *v* and *w*. As you
write the connecting stroke, don't let your bridge sag!

Day One — Practice the following letters and words from this week's Scripture.

Ff

God's

Follow

his

Day Two — Continue practicing letters and words from this week's Scripture.

Mm

imitates

much

child

Day Three   Practice the final letters and words from this week's Scripture.

Xx

example

everything

loved

Day Four   Practice this week's entire Scripture verse by tracing over each of the words below.

Follow God's example in everything you do just as a much loved child imitates his father.
Ephesians 5:1

FOR DISCUSSION
What are some good ways we might imitate God? Watch for opportunities to put these into practice!

Lesson 9

A train won't work unless it's on
the track. Keep your handwriting on track this
week by making sure your letters rest firmly on the line.

Day One Practice the following letters and words from this week's Scripture.

A a

have

Galatians

satisfaction

Day Two Continue practicing letters and words from this week's Scripture.

L l

personal

well

Let

Day Three — Practice the final letters and words from this week's Scripture.

Rr

work

sure

best

Day Four — Practice this week's entire Scripture verse by tracing over each of the words below.

Let everyone be sure that he
is doing his very best, for then he
will have the personal satisfaction
of work well done.

Galatians 6:4

FOR DISCUSSION

Why is it important to always do your very best? Make a list of some areas you'd like to improve in. Don't forget to ask God to help you!

TIP OF THE WEEK

This verse contains most of the overstroke letters (*m, n, v, y*). Think of some words that contain the other overstroke letters (*x* and *z*) and practice them, too!

Day One   Practice the following letters and words from this week's Scripture.

Mm

Most

important

makes

Day Two   Continue practicing letters and words from this week's Scripture.

Nn

continue

many

deep

Day Three   Practice the final letters and words from this week's Scripture.

Oo

other

show

faults

Day Four   Practice this week's entire Scripture verse by tracing over each of the words below.

Most important of all, continue
to show deep love for each other,
for love makes up for many of
your faults.

I Peter 4:8

FOR DISCUSSION
Why is it so important for Christians to love one another? (Hint: see John 13:34, 35.)

144

Lesson 11

TIP OF THE WEEK

Just like the capital *C*, the oval capital *E* begins just below
the top line. Also, remember that the forward oval capitals *B, P,*
and *R* begin with a flagstroke. (Notice the flagpole is leaning a bit!)

Day One   Practice the following letters and words from this week's Scripture.

Ee

each

given

abilities

Day Two   Continue practicing letters and words from this week's Scripture.

Pp

Peter

help

special

Day Three   Practice the final letters and words from this week's Scripture.

Ss

some

sure

use

Day Four   Practice this week's entire Scripture verse by tracing over each of the words below.

God has given each of you some special abilities; be sure to use them to help each other.

I Peter 4:10

FOR DISCUSSION

What special ability, knowledge, or talent has God given you? List some things that all of us can do to be helpful.

Name _____

Tip of the Week

The *H*, *J*, and *K*, are two-stroke capital letters.
There is also one three-stroke capital letter. Can you guess
what it is? (Here's a hint: It's just like a *J*, but with one stroke more.)

Day One Practice the following letters and words from this week's Scripture.

Hh

His

their

prayers

Day Two Continue practicing letters and words from this week's Scripture.

Ll

Lord

children

listening

Day Three Practice the final letters and words from this week's Scripture.

It

The

to

watching

Day Four Practice this week's entire Scripture verse by tracing over each of the words below.

The Lord is watching His children, listening to their prayers.
I Peter 3:12

FOR DISCUSSION
Having someone watch us can make us feel very good. But sometimes it makes us feel bad. What are some possible reasons for this?

TIP OF THE WEEK

The lowercase *g* and *q* are very similar. Be certain you
know which way the tail goes for each. The *q* is usually found
beside its best friend, the *u*. Practice the *qu* combination this week.

Day One Practice the following letters and words from this week's Scripture.

Bb

Be

beautiful

inside

Day Two Continue practicing letters and words from this week's Scripture.

Gg

gentle

lasting

precious

Qq

quiet

spirit

charm

Day Four   Practice this week's entire Scripture verse by tracing over each of the words below.

Be beautiful inside, in your hearts, with the lasting charm of a gentle and quiet spirit which is so precious to God.

I Peter 3:4

FOR DISCUSSION

Can someone be pretty on the outside, but ugly on the inside? How about the opposite? Explain.

Name _____

Lesson 14

TIP OF THE WEEK

Everyone's name is special. You may be named
after a relative, or family friend, or something totally unique!
Be proud of your name and write it so anyone can read it!

Day One Practice the following letters and words from this week's Scripture.

Oo

loving

one

toward

Day Two Continue practicing letters and words from this week's Scripture.

Uu

humble

should

tender

Day Three
Practice the final letters and words from this week's Scripture.

Yy

family

sympathy

minds

Day Four
Practice this week's entire Scripture verse by tracing over each of the words below.

You should be like one big happy family, full of sympathy toward each other, loving one another with tender hearts and humble minds.

I Peter 3:8

FOR DISCUSSION
When someone you care about feels bad, do you feel bad, too? How does this relate to our Scripture verse this week?

Name _____

Tip of the Week

There are two dotted letters this week — the *i* and *j*.
Add a small dot (not a circle) after you finish the word. Also,
check your lowercase *e*'s to make sure they don't look like *i*'s.

Day One Practice the following letters and words from this week's Scripture.

Ff

fellowship

wonderful

we

Day Two Continue practicing letters and words from this week's Scripture.

Li

Lf

light

living

Day Three
Practice the final letters and words from this week's Scripture.

Jj

John

joy

presence

Day Four
Practice this week's entire Scripture verse by tracing over each of the words below.

If we are living in the light of God's presence...we have wonderful fellowship and joy with each other.

I John 1:7

FOR DISCUSSION
According to this verse, how does our relationship with God affect the way we relate to each other? Explain.

TIP OF THE WEEK

Your lowercase oval letters (*a, c, d, g, o,* and *q*) should
be round and smooth, not squashed like someone sat on them!
To look its best, the oval part of each letter should fill the middle space.

Day One Practice the following letters and words from this week's Scripture.

Aa

snap

are

at

Day Two Continue practicing letters and words from this week's Scripture.

Dd

Don't

unkind

evil

Day Three
Practice the final letters and words from this week's Scripture.

Rr

repay

those

back

Day Four
Practice this week's entire Scripture verse by tracing over each of the words below.

Don't repay evil for evil. Don't snap back at those who say unkind things about you. We are to be kind to others, and God will bless us for it.

I Peter 3:9

FOR DISCUSSION
How should you act when someone is being unkind? What should be our attitude toward those who are mean to us? (Hint: see Luke 23:34.)

Name _____

📚 **TIP OF THE WEEK**

Just as you need space between a classmate's desk and
your desk, words also need a letter space between them for easier
reading. Wordsthataretooclosetogether are much too hard to read!

Day One   Practice the following letters and words from this week's Scripture.

Hh

home

within

that

Day Two   Continue practicing letters and words from this week's Scripture.

Ss

hearts

as

trust

Uv

living

more

pray

Day Four   Practice this week's entire Scripture verse by tracing over each of the words below.

I pray that Christ will be
more and more at home in your
hearts, living within you as you
trust in Him.

Ephesians 3:17

FOR DISCUSSION

What does it mean to make someone "feel at home?" Describe the kind of heart where Jesus could feel at home.

TIP OF THE WEEK

Look for similarities and differences between the
lowercase *u -w,* and the *m -n*. Make certain you write
these letters clearly and carefully so they can't be mistaken for each other.

Day One Practice the following letters and words from this week's Scripture.

Nn

and

then

wants

Day Two Continue practicing letters and words from this week's Scripture.

Pp

Philippians

helping

obey

Practice the final letters and words from this week's Scripture.

Ww

want

work

what

Practice this week's entire Scripture verse by tracing over each of the words below.

God is at work within you, helping you want to obey Him, and then helping you do what He wants.

Philippians 2:13

FOR DISCUSSION

Where does this verse say the desire to obey comes from? List some ways that we can become closer to God.

TIP OF THE WEEK

Look for similarities and differences between
the lowercase *h* and *k*. Like the lowercase *u - w* and
m - n, these letters must be written clearly to avoid mistakes in reading.

Day One Practice the following letters and words from this week's Scripture.

Bb

bring

be

child

Day Two Continue practicing letters and words from this week's Scripture.

Gg

good

glory

which

Day Three — Practice the final letters and words from this week's Scripture.

Kk

kind

doing

praise

Day Four — Practice this week's entire Scripture verse by tracing over each of the words below.

May you always be doing those good, kind things which show that you are a child of God, for this will bring much praise and glory to the Lord.

Philippians 1:11

FOR DISCUSSION

List some ways we can help our neighbors. How does our kind behavior affect what people think about Christians?

Name _____

📚 TIP OF THE WEEK

Have you looked at the "stars" lately? The **Five Star** evaluation can help you determine areas in your handwriting that need work. Watch your alignment, shape, size, slant and spacing.

Day One Practice the following letters and words from this week's Scripture.

Dd

grudges

ready

hold

Day Two Continue practicing letters and words from this week's Scripture.

Ee

Remember

gentle

never

Ff

forgave

forgive

must

Day Four Practice this week's entire Scripture verse by tracing over each of the words below.

Be gentle and ready to forgive; never hold grudges. Remember, the Lord forgave you, so you must forgive others.

Colossians 3:13

FOR DISCUSSION

How can holding a grudge be harmful? Why do you think forgiving each other is important?

Name _____

TIP OF THE WEEK

Some of us look a lot like our parents. Some capital and lowercase pairs look alike, too. The *Cc* is one such pair. Also look at the *Aa, Xx, Yy, Jy*.

Day One Practice the following letters and words from this week's Scripture.

Cc

Colossians

church

perfect

Day Two Continue practicing letters and words from this week's Scripture.

Ll

life

let

whole

Day Three — Practice the final letters and words from this week's Scripture.

Mm

Most

harmony

all

Day Four — Practice this week's entire Scripture verse by tracing over each of the words below.

Most of all, let love guide your life, for then the whole church will stay together in perfect harmony.

Colossians 3:14

FOR DISCUSSION
If you really love everyone, how might it affect your behavior? List some ways you can let love guide your life.

TIP OF THE WEEK

To help you remember the correct strokes,
Sky Write the capital letters from this lesson (*I, J,* and *Q*)
and see if a classmate can tell which one you're writing.

Day One Practice the following letters and words from this week's Scripture.

Ii

first

loving

comes

Day Two Continue practicing letters and words from this week's Scripture.

Jj

James

peace

pure

Qq

quiet

heaven

gentleness

Day Four   Practice this week's entire Scripture verse by tracing over each of the words below.

But the wisdom that comes from heaven is first of all pure and full of quiet gentleness. Then it is peace—loving and courteous.
—James 3:17

FOR DISCUSSION

Think of someone who seems "full of quiet gentleness." How do you think they became that kind of person?

TIP OF THE WEEK

Check your posture. It's amazing how much of a
difference correct posture can make in your handwriting. Also,
make sure your paper is going the same direction as your writing arm.

Day One   Practice the following letters and words from this week's Scripture.

Kk

making

make

other's

Day Two   Continue practicing letters and words from this week's Scripture.

Uu

faults

because

each

Day Three
Practice the final letters and words from this week's Scripture.

Xx

exception

allowance

patient

Day Four
Practice this week's entire Scripture verse by tracing over each of the words below.

Be patient with each other, making allowance for each other's faults because of your love.

Ephesians 4:2

FOR DISCUSSION
Have you ever been impatient with someone, or critical? How can we learn to make allowances for another's weaknesses?

Name _____

TIP OF THE WEEK

The apostrophe *s* on *God's* means we belong to God —
we're part of God's family! You can share with the rest of God's family
by giving your Scripture Border Sheet this week to someone new.

Day One   Practice the following letters and words from this week's Scripture.

Cc

Christian

country

belong

Day Two   Continue practicing letters and words from this week's Scripture.

Yy
You

family

members

Day Three — Practice the final letters and words from this week's Scripture.

Zz

citizens

household

God's

Day Four — Practice this week's entire Scripture verse by tracing over each of the words below.

You are members of God's very own family, citizens of God's country, and you belong in God's household with every other Christian.

Ephesians 2:19

FOR DISCUSSION

Isn't it great to be part of God's family?
List some ways you can share
God's love with others.

LOW FAT MILK 99¢

TIP OF THE WEEK

Make sure your letters are "planted" in
the right space. Your tail letters need to touch the
bottom line, and your tall letters need to reach the top line.

Day One Practice the following letters and words from this week's Scripture.

Mm

May

marvelous

high

Day Two Continue practicing letters and words from this week's Scripture.

Oo

down

soil

roots

Day Three Practice the final letters and words from this week's Scripture.

Ww

how

wide

understand

Day Four Practice this week's entire Scripture verse by tracing over each of the words below.

May your roots go down deep into the soil of God's marvelous love; and may you be able to feel and understand...how long, how wide, how deep, and how high His love really is.

Ephesians 3:17-19

FOR DISCUSSION

What do you think this verse means when it says our "roots" should "go down deep" into God's love? Explain.

TIP OF THE WEEK

Remember, to help you write more rapidly
and smoothly, be sure to dot your *i*'s and cross your *t*'s
after you finish the entire word. The same is true for *j*'s and *x*'s, too.

Day One — Practice the following letters and words from this week's Scripture.

Gg

God

bring

understanding

Day Two — Continue practicing letters and words from this week's Scripture.

Rr

ever

deeper

from

Tt

Thessalonians

patience

into

Day Four Practice this week's entire Scripture verse by tracing over each of the words below.

May the Lord bring you into an ever deeper understanding of the love of God and of the patience that comes from Christ.

II Thessalonians 3:5

FOR DISCUSSION

What have you learned about the love of God this year? Why not share your new insights with a friend?

Name _____

Tip of the week
Always look for the good in
each other. Trade papers with a classmate,
then point out each other's best letters and words.

Day One   Practice the following letters and words from this week's Scripture.

A a

about

against

law

Day Two   Continue practicing letters and words from this week's Scripture.

D d

do

dear

another

Day Three   Practice the final letters and words from this week's Scripture.

Zz

criticize

speak

brothers

Day Four   Practice this week's entire Scripture verse by tracing over each of the words below.

Don't criticize and speak evil about each other, dear brothers. If you do, you will be fighting against God's law of loving one another.

James 4:11

FOR DISCUSSION

Compare this verse with Ephesians 4:2 (see lesson 23). How are they different? How are they similar?

To The Teacher

The following pages are for use on Day 5 of the Weekly Lesson Format (see Teacher Guidebook, page 56).

These Scripture Border Sheets not only provide a significant outreach component, but a strong motivational tool as well.

This section contains 30 Scripture Border Sheets — one per lesson, plus an extra, plus two blanks (at the end of this section) that allow for student-designed artwork.

Since this *Transition Student Workbook* contains both manuscript and cursive lessons, each Border Sheet offers two line sizes. Right-hand pages have lines suitable for manuscript lessons; left-hand pages have lines appropriate for cursive lessons. (Note: If students plan to give Border Sheets as gifts, they may wish to glue the finished sheets to construction paper to hide the reverse side.)

For creative ways to use the Scripture Border Sheets, see "Ways to Share" (Teacher Guidebook, page 58).

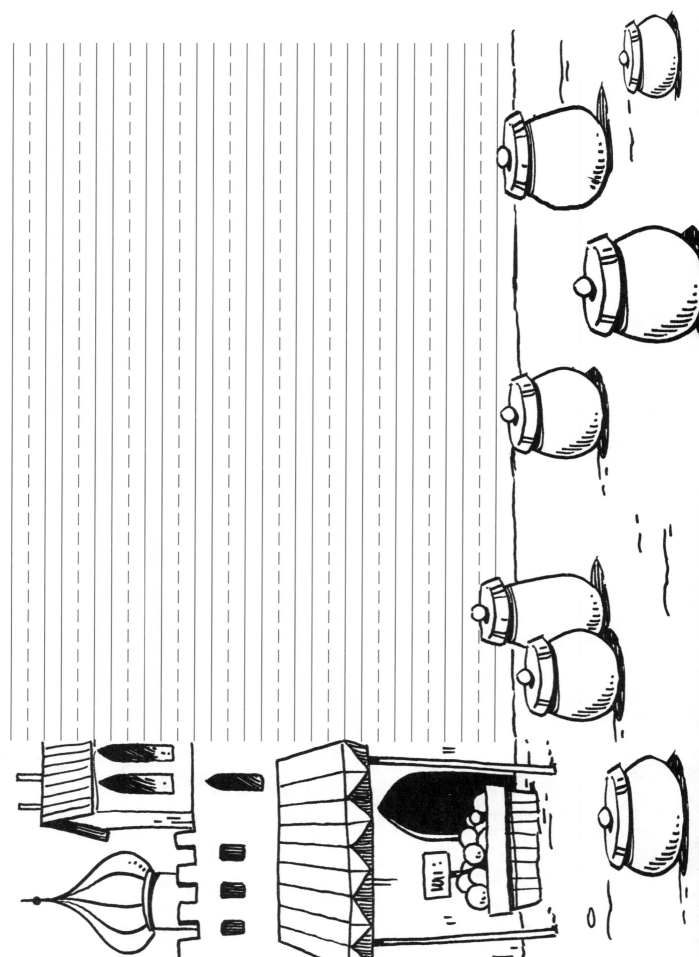

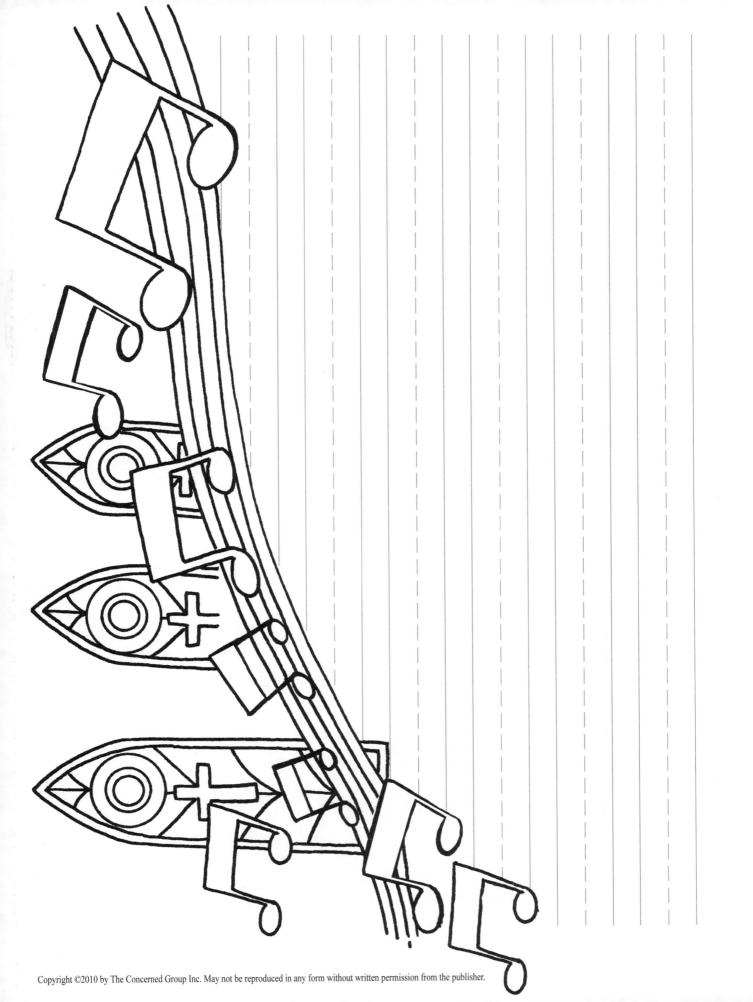

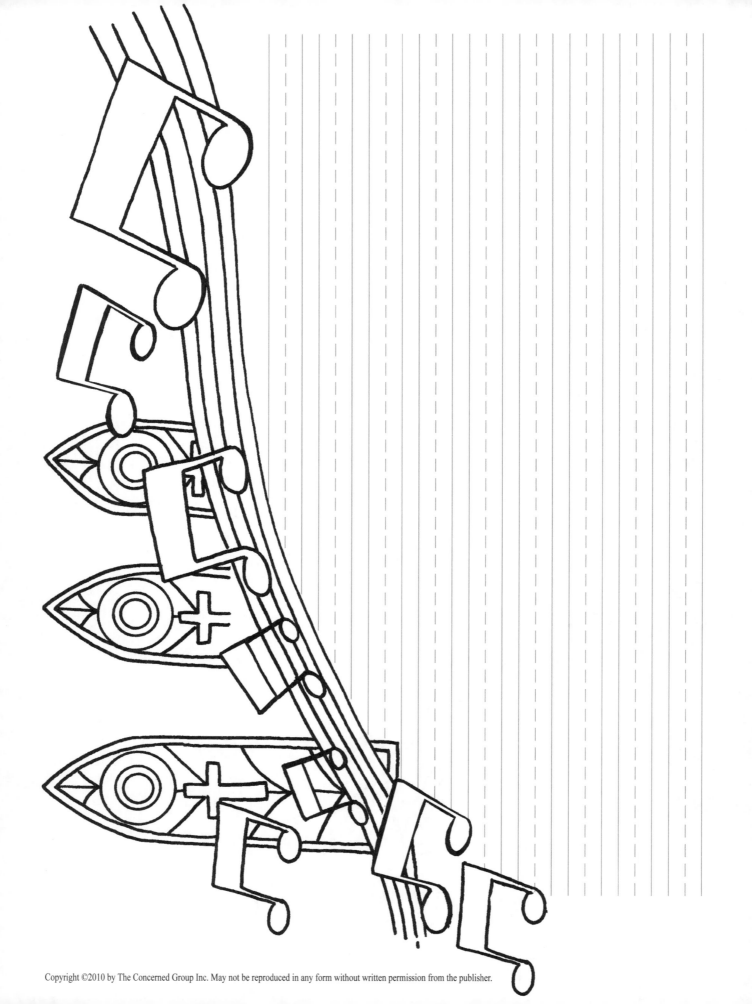

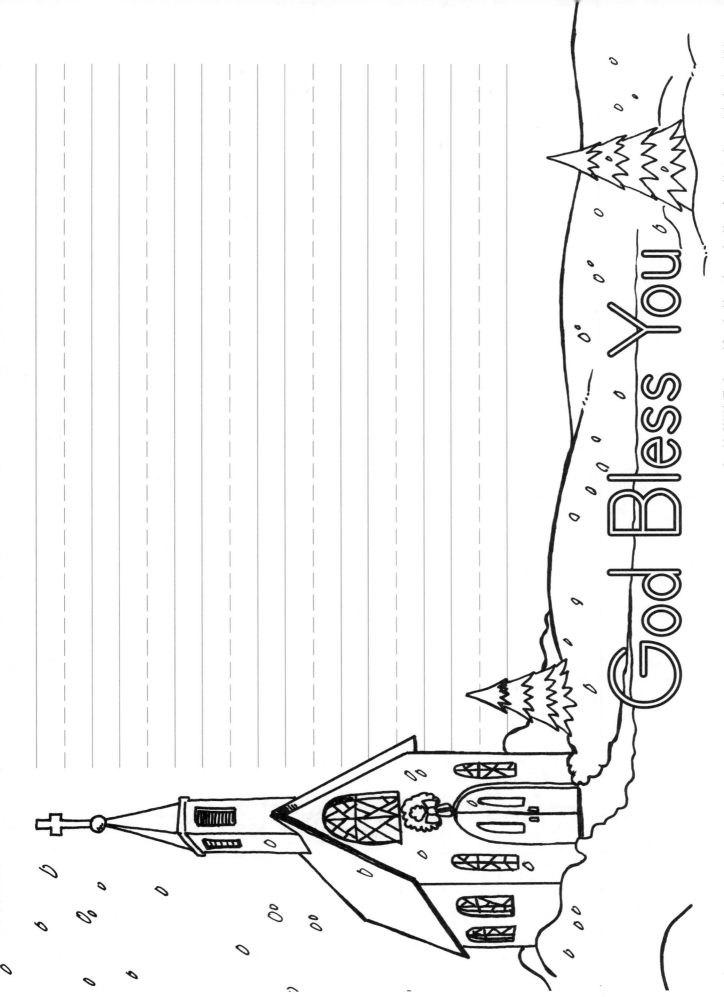

God Bless You

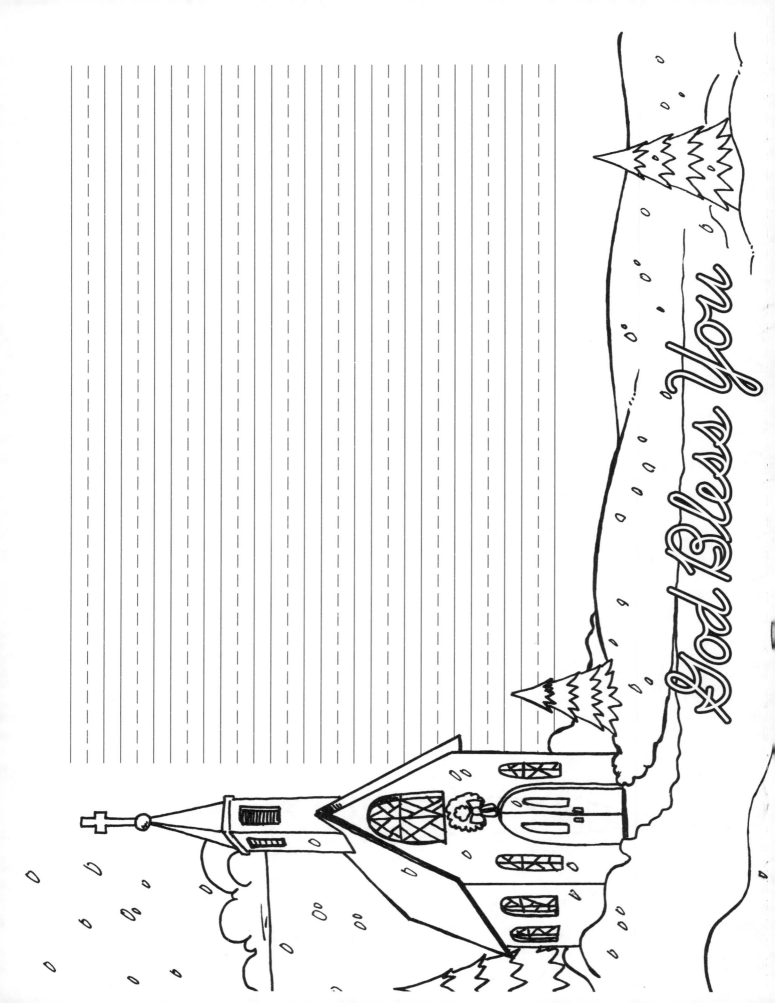

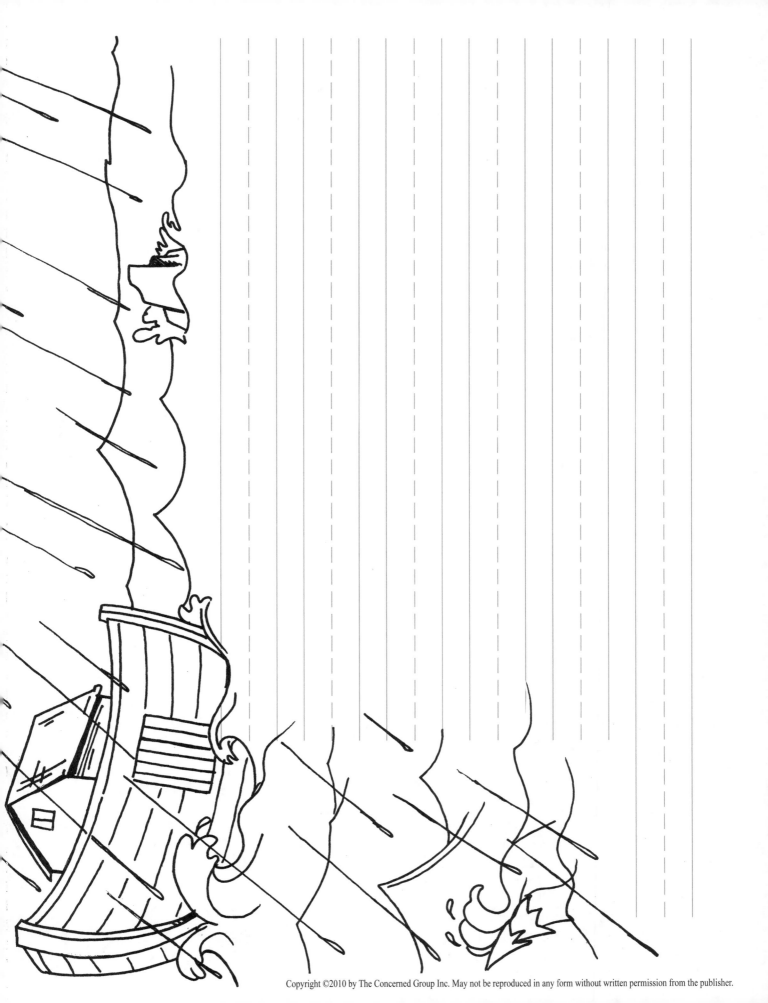

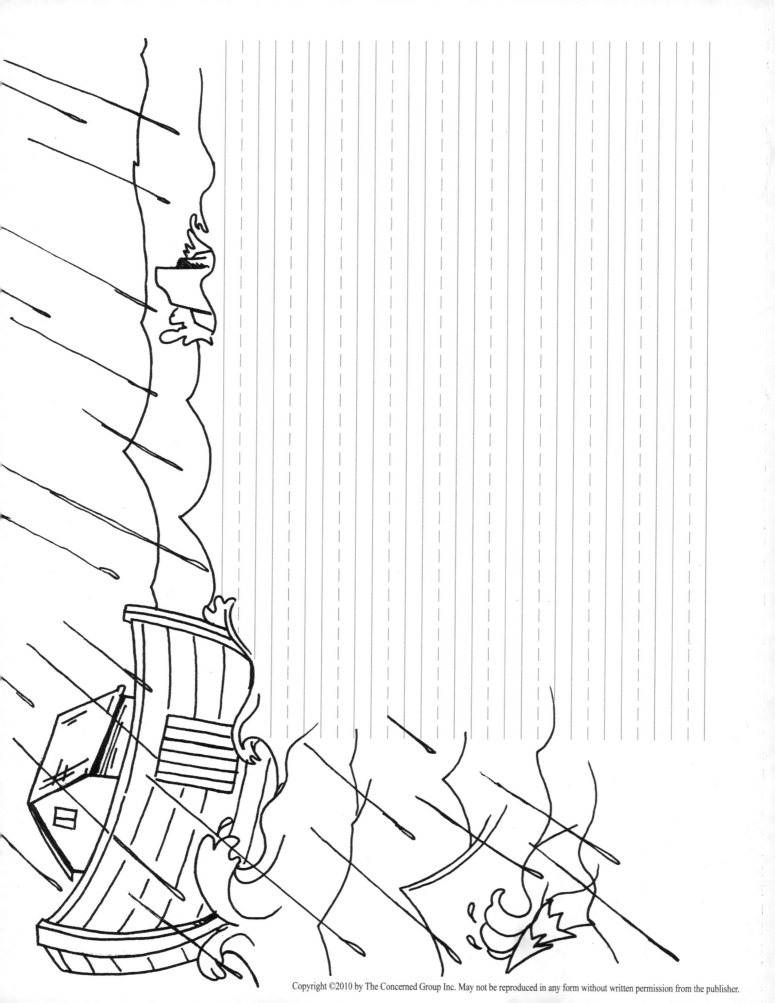

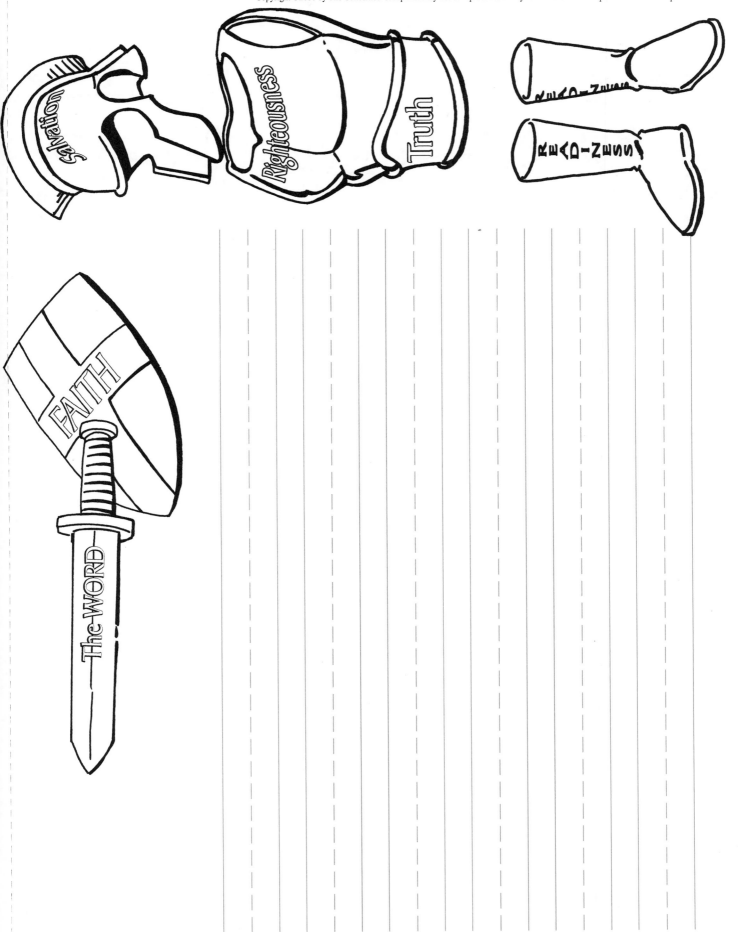

Salvation

Righteousness

Truth

FAITH

The WORD

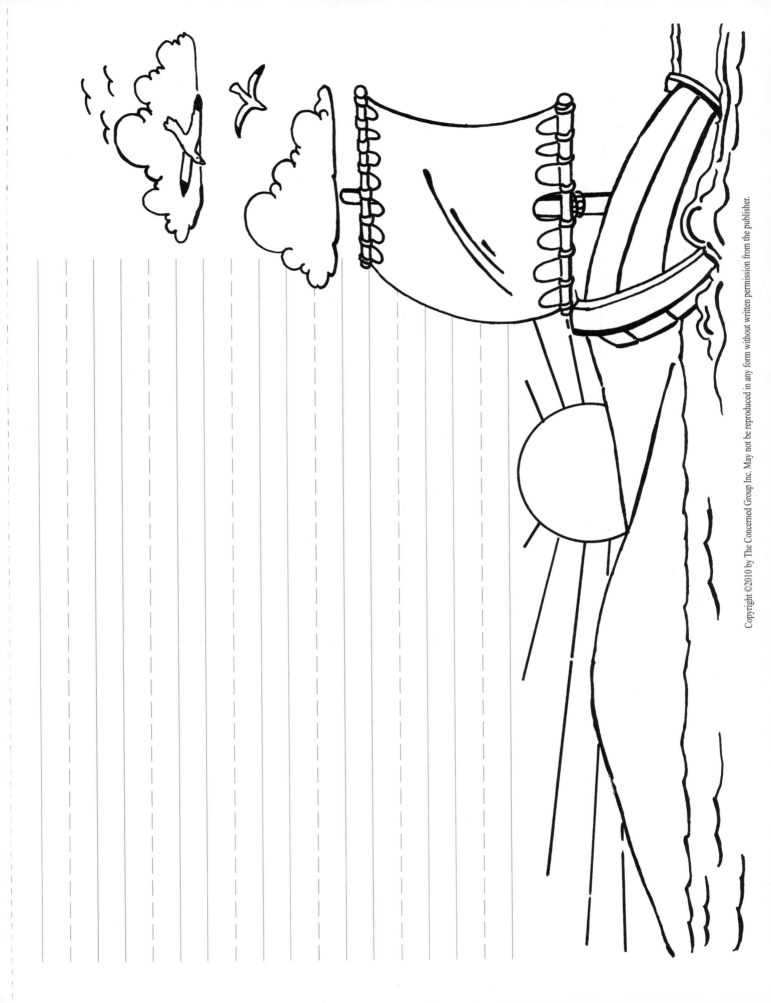

Copyright ©2010 by The Concerned Group Inc. May not be reproduced in any form without written permission from the publisher.

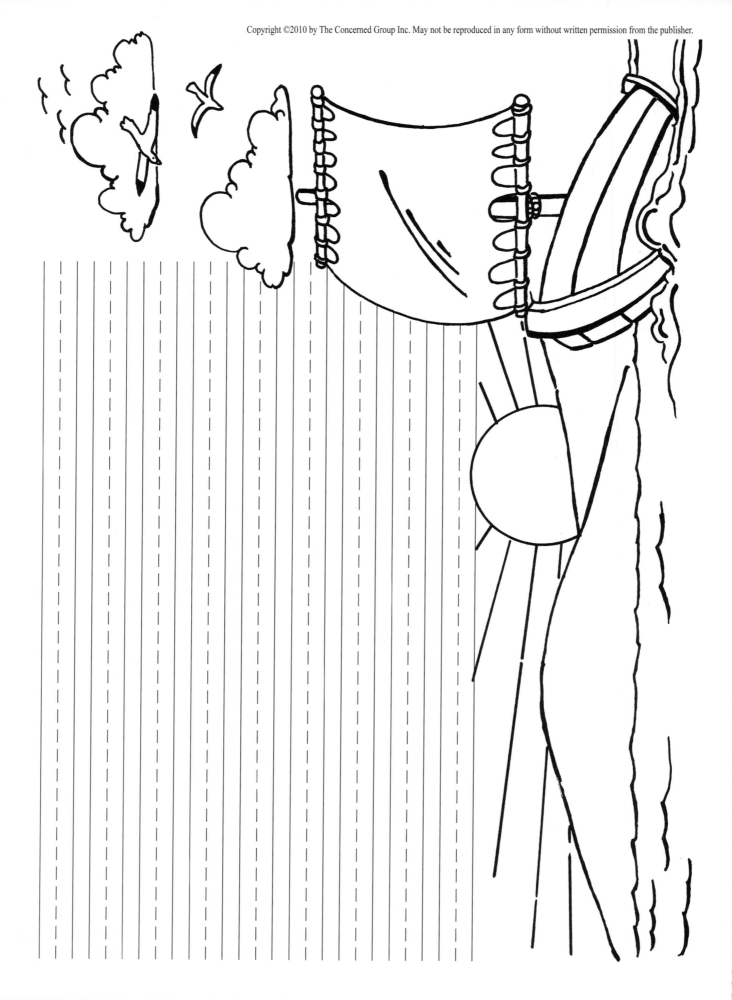

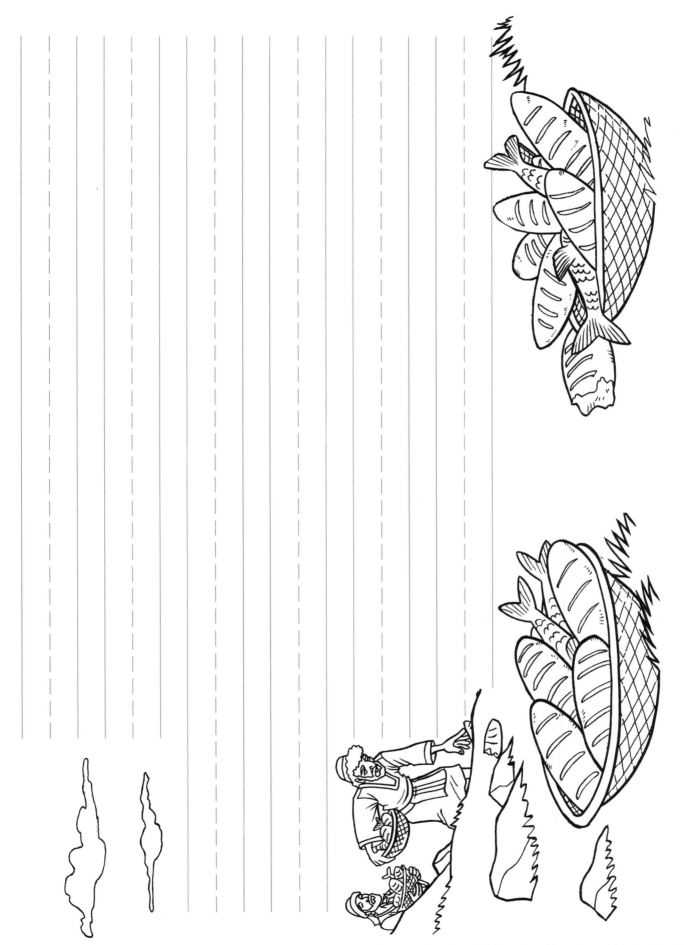

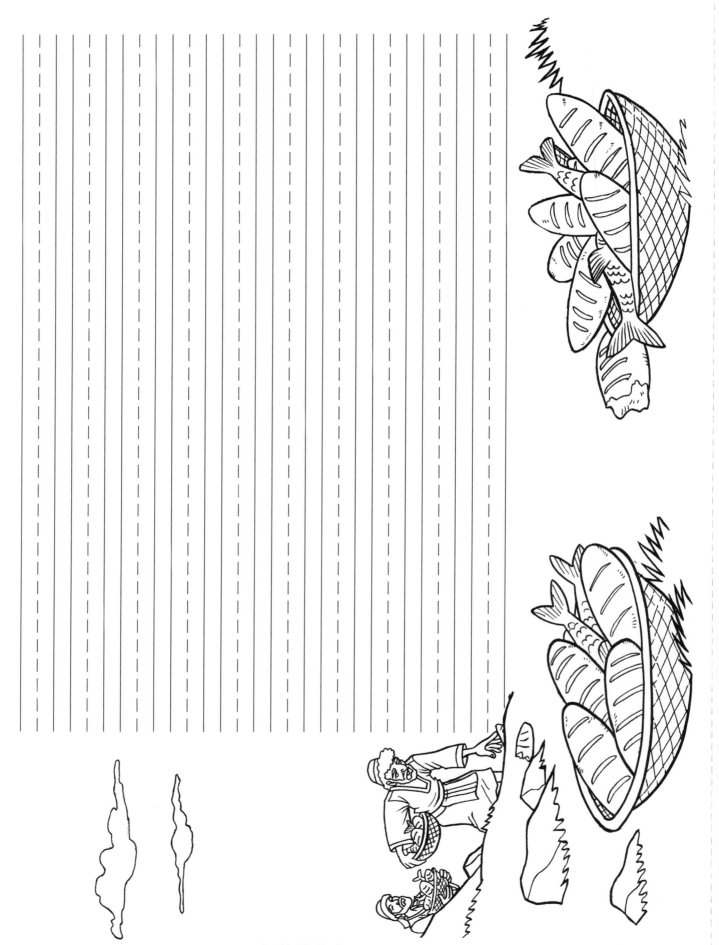

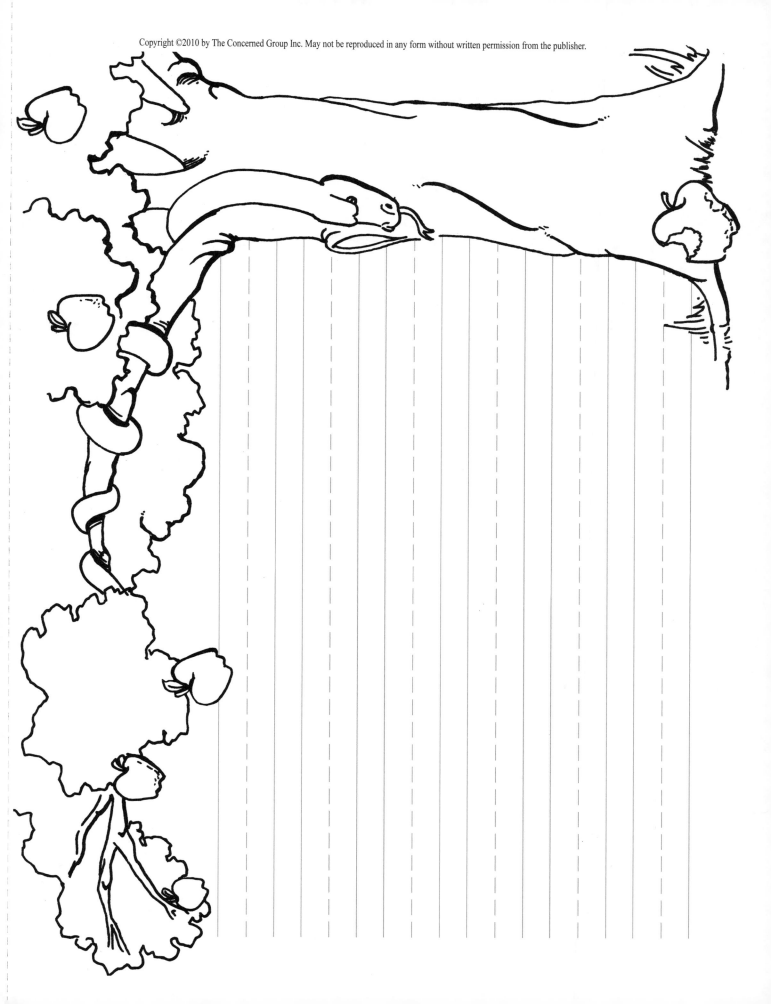

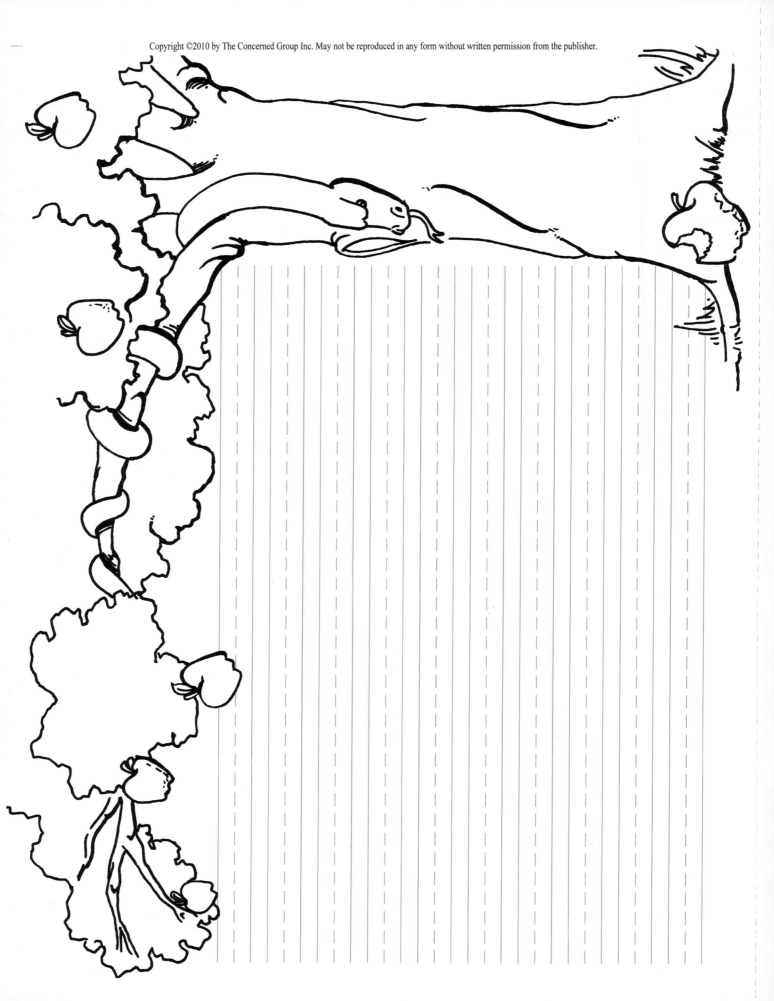

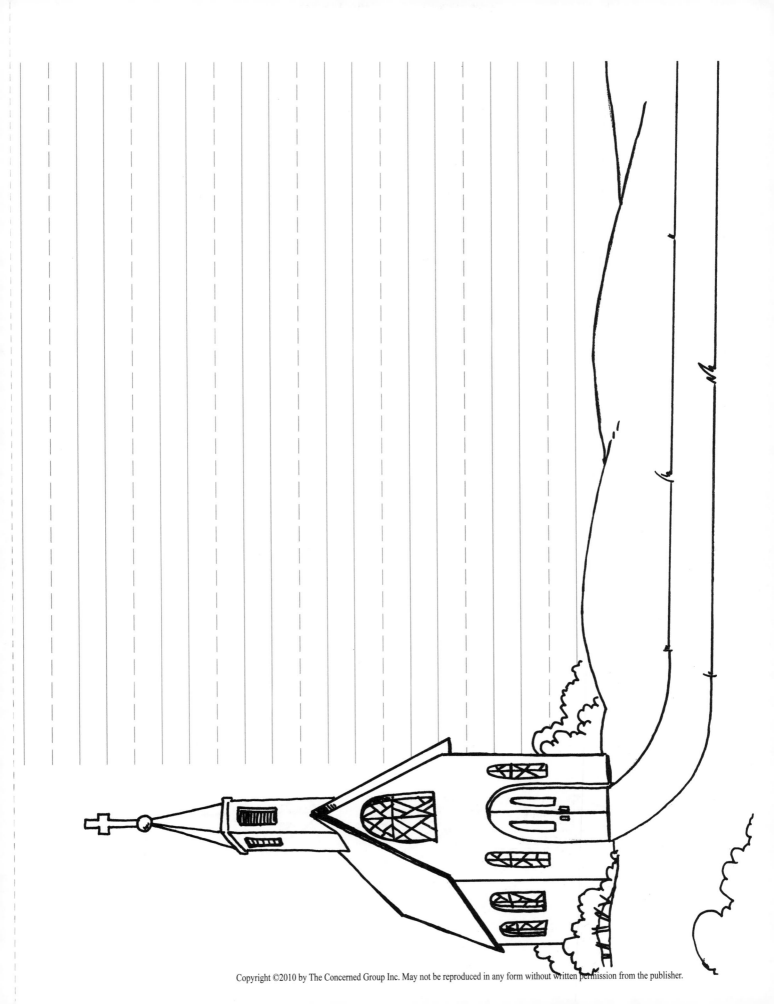

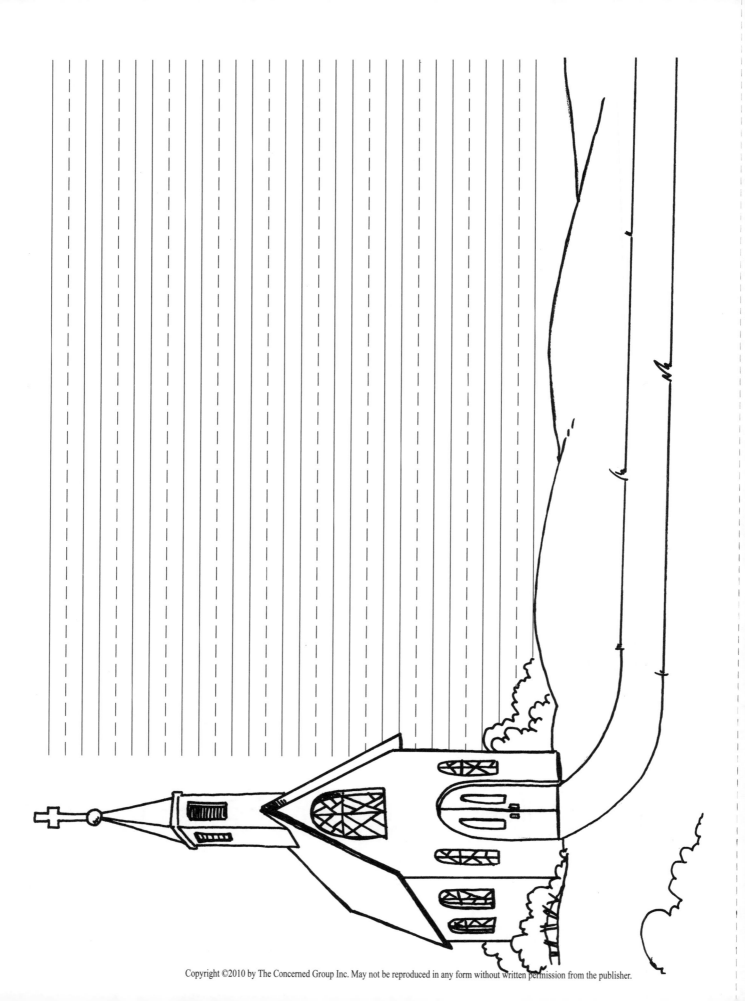

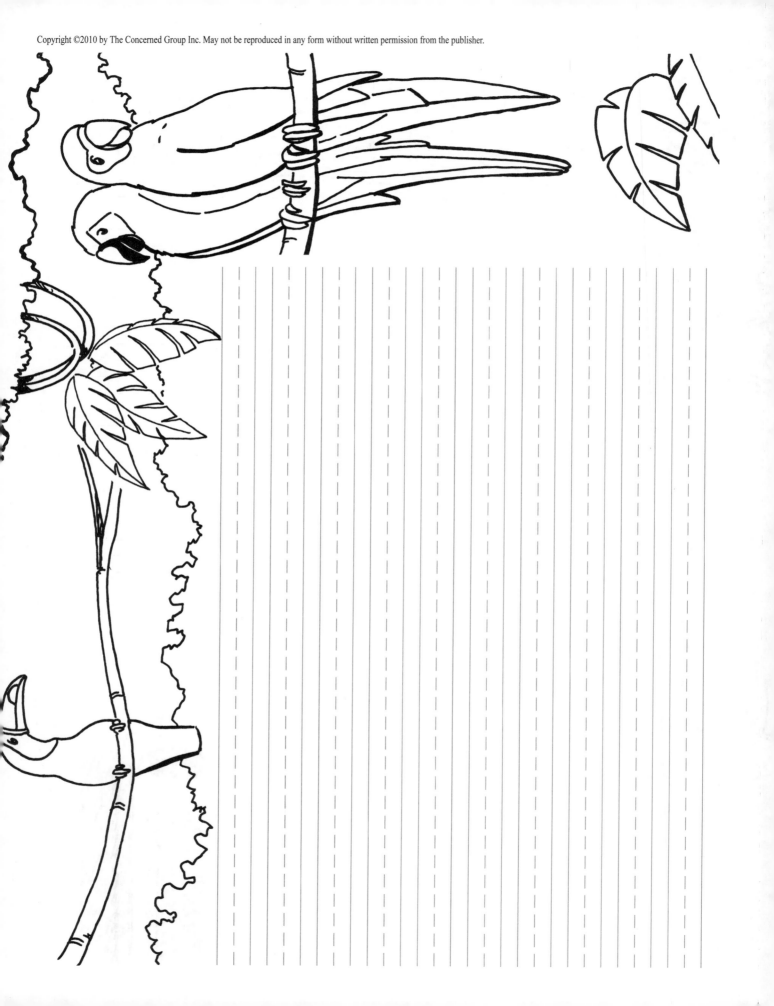

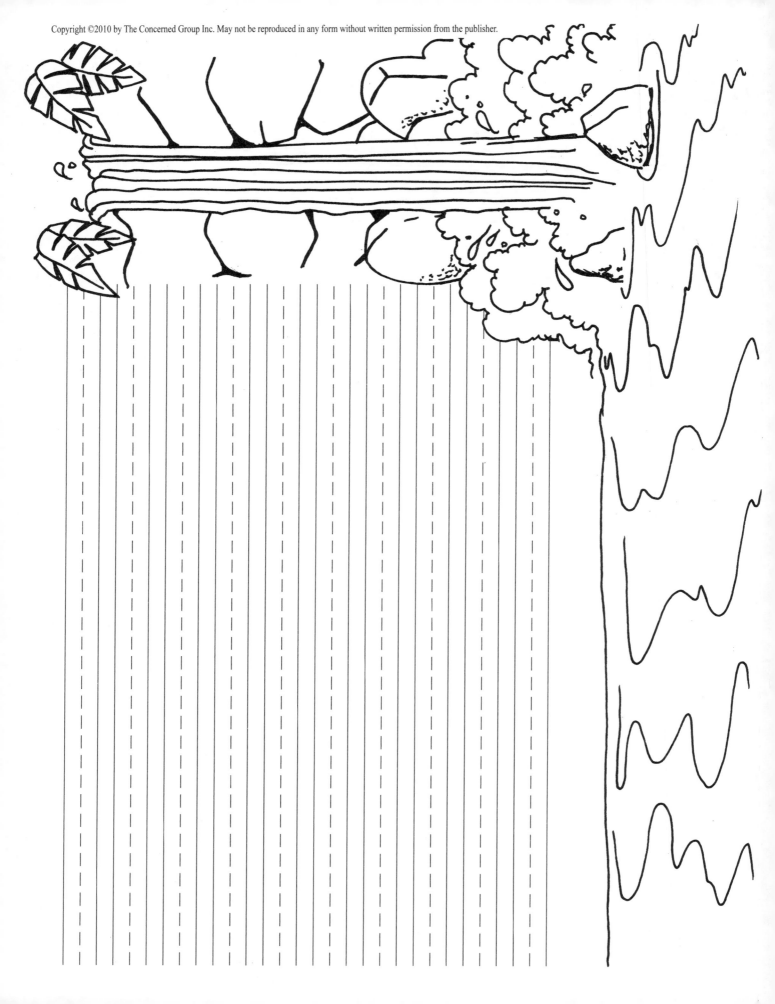

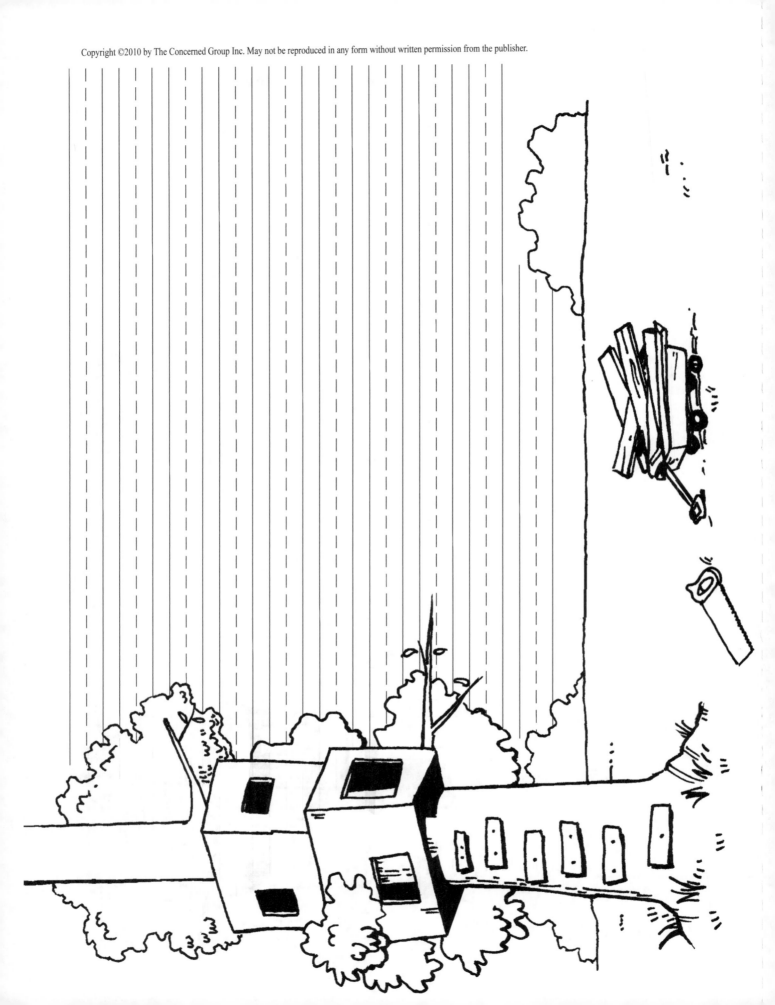

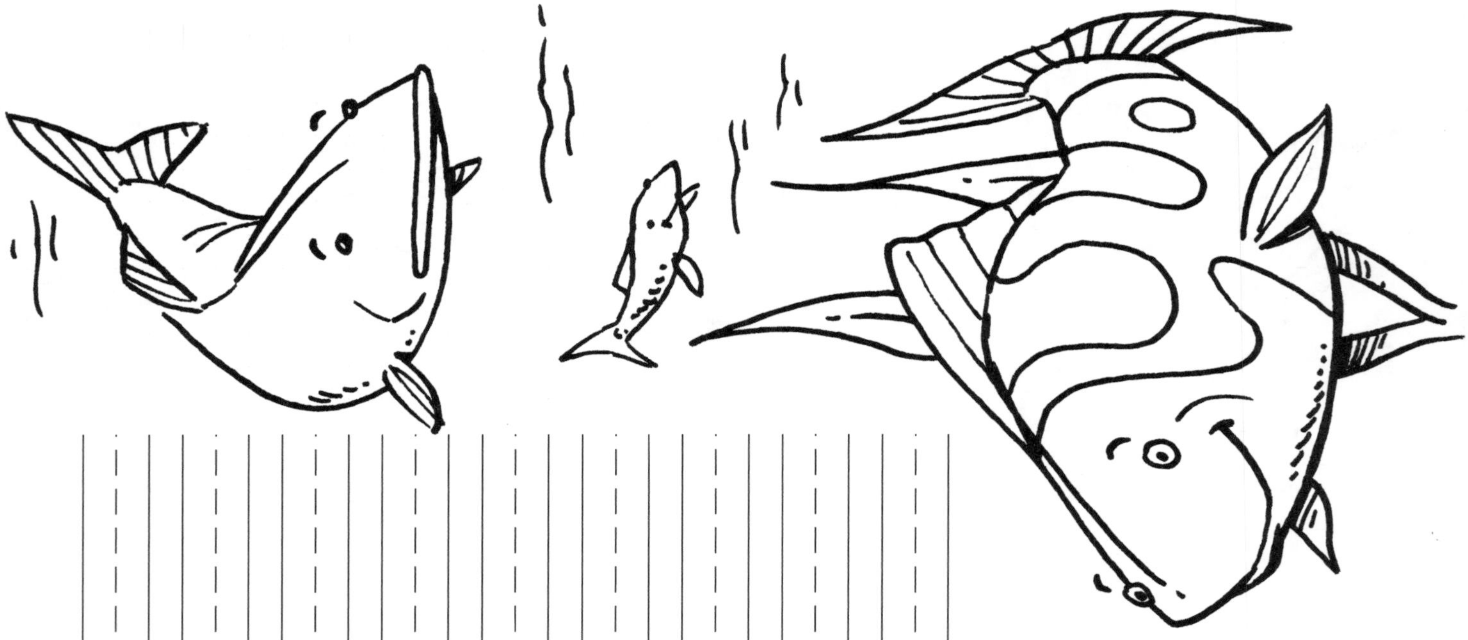

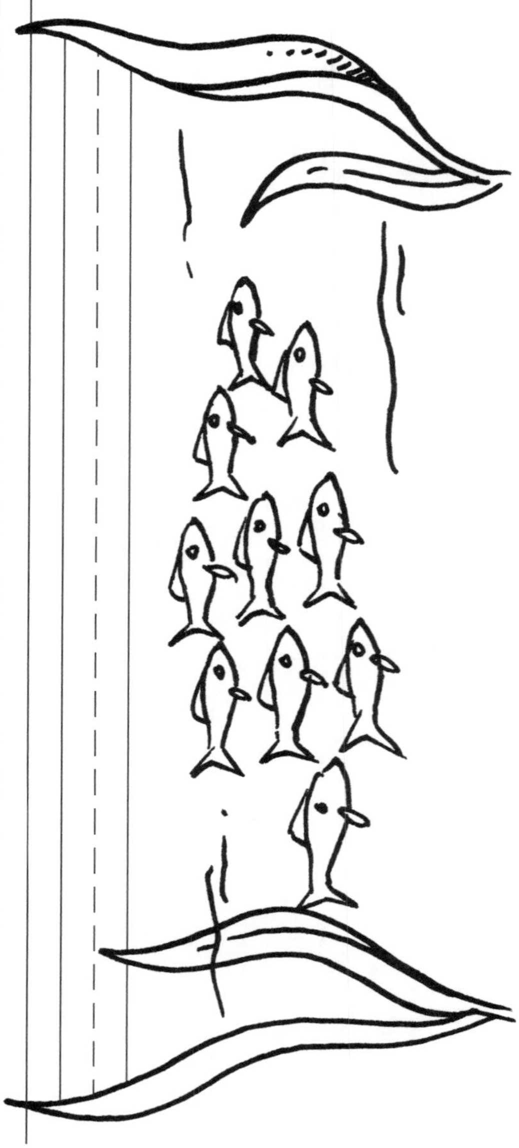

Copyright ©2010 by The Concerned Group Inc. May not be reproduced in any form without written permission from the publisher.

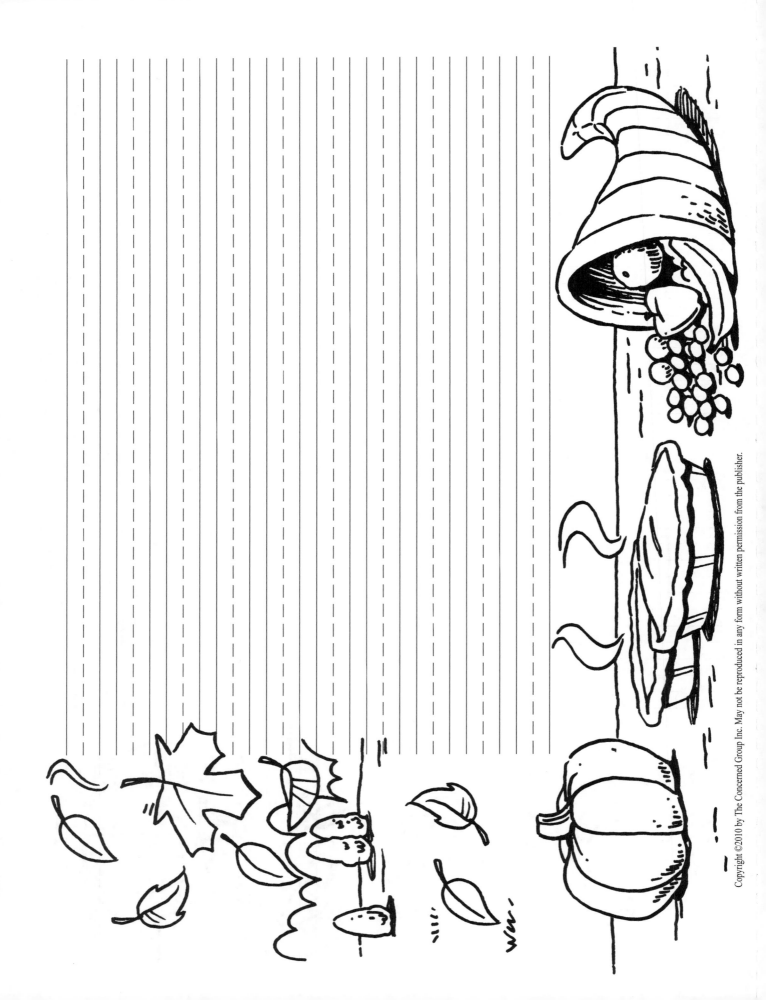